HOCKEY IS MY LIFE

HOCKEY

IS

MY LIFE

Phil Esposito
with Gerald Eskenazi

Illustrated with photographs

DODD, MEAD & COMPANY • NEW YORK

ISBN: 0-396-06700-X
Library of Congress Catalog Card Number: 72-3927
Printed in the United States of America
by The Cornwall Press, Inc., Cornwall, N. Y.

*To all those in the world
of professional hockey*

Editor's Foreword

A reporter doesn't always enjoy the luxury of being a fan. Naturally I'm partial to certain teams and players, but I always try to remain objective in my reporting.

For a variety of reasons, I like watching the Bruins. They seem to have a good time on the ice. Their players are loose, verbal, and cooperative in the dressing room, their coaches unusually honest.

Over the past six months I've been able to talk about some interesting characters with Phil Esposito—an interesting character himself. Here is a man whose records simply defy any normal standards of measurement. Yet there is much more to a person than his performance on the playing field. So I set out to learn from this man about the headaches of the game, the strain and pressures, and also the fun. I wanted to hear stories out of school. I wanted to know the pleasures of sipping champagne from the Stanley Cup. But most of all, I wanted an honest book about a truly exciting sport that only in the last few years has achieved any sort of general acceptance in the United States.

I'd only seen two or three hockey games before my newspaper asked me to cover the season's opener in Boston in 1964 between the Bruins and the Rangers. I forget who won. The final score was something like 9–4; and Reg Fleming, then with Boston, mopped up several New York players. Later he was to be their teammate.

This violence on a 200 x 85 foot frozen surface intrigued me. The speed of the game, the condition of the athletes, the perpetual drama—all these factors make hockey thrilling to watch and a pleasure to write about. Sure, the season is too long and, yes, the quality of play is frequently dreadful because of continuous dilution. Yet, every second of each game is poundingly different. There are no expectations. Everything is a surprise.

In preparing this book I'm grateful to Fred Sharf, a Cantab who somehow wandered into Boston Garden one day and wound up as Phil's business partner. From the beginning Fred was enthusiastic about this operation, which he approached as scientifically, and with as many notes, as he must have his Ph.D. thesis in business administration. Also to Peter Weed, a rink habitué and editor, who was instrumental in blending the thoughts of a man from Sault Ste. Marie (Phil) and one from Brooklyn (me).

Although she can't type, Roz Eskenazi has a unique ability to assist me in such a project. Maybe it's her dinners, which never got cold.

—GERALD ESKENAZI

New York, September 1972

Contents

HOCKEY IS MY LIFE

1

Making It

I'm a high school dropout.

I'm also a hockey player making six figures a year, with a corporation doing a multimillion-dollar business. Maybe I'm lucky. Maybe I'm a little smart and a little good. But I look around at my sport sometimes and I think of all the guys who dropped out, like me, who are slaving in the steel mill back home in Sault Ste. Marie, or who are scrounging a living after their playing days are over. One guy I used to play with calls himself an interior decorator. He's a house painter.

First off, I've got to say this: the National Hockey League has been good to me. The Boston Bruins have been good to me. I'm not driving a truck for the mill, and that's something. But I've never fooled myself for one minute either. Hockey became a job for me the day I signed my first pro contract. If a professional athlete can't cut it, who needs him. Life's like that. You'd think it should be different in sports, but it isn't. This is a hard life, and if you don't produce you're no good to the team. That's what it's all about, isn't it? What you do for them?

Yet, there's a revolution going on in hockey. We're the last sport to be touched by it. For years we sat back and watched basketball, football, and baseball players haul down the big salaries for doing a job that no self-respecting hockey player really feels is as difficult. This revolution in my sport isn't being brought about by strikes or picketing or phoney threats of jumping to another league. It's here because (1) we're smarter and (2) they need us.

I made it to the NHL in 1963. I'd cut school short like practically everyone else playing hockey. When I came up, 75 percent of the NHL players hadn't graduated from high school. What the heck did we know about contracts? Nothing. What did we know about negotiating with a general manager who's been around 20 years and has only one thought in mind: getting this kid as cheap as possible? And another thing—we were frightened. When you're a high school dropout and all you know is playing hockey— well, brother, you sign. I envy the kids today. Sure, I know that Fred Shero criticized them when he took over the Philadelphia Flyers in 1971. "What's a kid got to worry about these days?" said Shero. "They know that if they don't make it with a club they'll wind up someplace else in the league." What's wrong with that? It's about time the players had something to say about where they'd like to play.

I'll give you an idea of how rough it is for a kid. We had a rookie with us not long ago, a real good kid. But what did he know about reading contracts? You put something in front of him and he signs it. Well, before he signed his contract he asked me for advice. I turned him over to my business partner, Fred Sharf. The kid read something in the contract to Fred, but couldn't pronounce a word. Fred was shocked. The word was "negotiate." Now, how's a kid supposed to negotiate if he doesn't even know what the word means?

At least this particular player had someone to ask. When I was talking about money no one even thought about lawyers or agents or business representatives. I think management would have passed out if I'd said, "Hey, let me ask my advisor about this clause."

The way up for my generation was the same way for previous generations. You played hockey from the time you first learned to cross the street by yourself. Then you played and played. You hooked up with the local team, moving up the ladder as you got older and better. So far, so good. Not much different from the way the kids do it in the States with their sports. But then things changed. You see, in Canada the big-league clubs owned most of the good junior teams. And if you wanted to move up in hockey, you had to play for a junior squad; it was the training ground. Once you played for a junior team, and it was sponsored by an NHL club, then for the rest of your career you belonged to the NHL team.

That didn't matter to most of us back in the Soo. You

wanted to get to the big time. When I was 13 all I could think of was skating. The best bantam team was the Algoma Contractors, sponsored by the mining outfit where my father was a foreman. Every October the Contractors held a tryout run by Angelo Bombacco, their coach. By then enough natural ice had formed in Central Park. About 60 boys would try out for the team. The day would start at 9 in the morning and end at 6 at night. Sometimes it was 25° below with a stiff wind blowing.

I was bigger than most of the other kids. Gangly and awkward. My muscles hadn't developed enough to support my size. Still, I tried. I worked like hell to make the team. I knew I could stickhandle better than anyone. The trouble was, I first had to get the puck. When the tryout was over Bombacco motioned 20 boys to one side of the ice. They were to be his team. I was on the other side, among the losers. Later in the dressing room I cried. I've never forgotten that day. Even now when I go back to the Soo I remind Angelo about it, and we have a good laugh. But at the time, I was crushed.

Luckily I hooked on with another team, the Sportsman's Bantams. After a few months I got into the groove. Everything started to work for me. We played the Contractors that Christmas; I scored a few goals against them; and we won. Needless to say, I was delighted.

Big men take time to get rolling. And this being a slow-starter would occasionally haunt me in later years. But the next year I made the Contractors.

It was hard work to stay on the club. I had no coordination and Bombacco took me to a doctor to see what he could suggest. The prescription: gymnastics. In addition to being poorly coordinated, I had this ridiculous habit of falling like a tree. I just didn't know how to land properly. I fell so often and so hard that my body was covered with bruises. Every time I hit the ice I was in danger. So the trainer sewed sponges into my pants to protect my hips, which got it the worst.

The Contractors were a powerhouse. Yet, any loss would send me into a depression. If the club won 10 in a row and lost its next game I'd be upset. My body and mind were wrapped up in hockey to the point of exhaustion. I'd play my regular shifts, then kill penalties and also operate on the power play. There was a game I remember for the Northern Ontario Hockey Association championship. I saw triple duty and got three goals. We were a happy bunch as we went into a local diner for something to eat. I ordered my food. Before it arrived I fell asleep.

The next few years I moved up the ladder—to the midget division and then to the juvenile ranks. With each new team I had to prove myself again. I continued to have poor training camps. Yet, I'd win more than my share of honors. So the next logical step for me was the juniors and, since there was no junior team nearby, that meant I would have to leave home.

Bombacco had done some scouting for the Chicago Black Hawks and had contacts with the Hawks' top Junior A club, the St. Catherine Tepees (later to become the Black Hawks). Chicago was rebuilding its organization and looking for all the top players they could find. The team had never finished first in the NHL, and was said to have been inflicted by the Muldoon Curse. This curse was supposed to have started in 1927 when Pete Muldoon, their first coach, was fired. That day he said, "The Chicago Black Hawks will never finish first in the National Hockey League." But now in the sixties the Black Hawks were trying their damndest to do so. Angelo knew they were looking for big, strong, young players. He also realized, though, that it took time for me to catch someone's eye. No one was going to do cartwheels the first day they saw me at training camp. He decided that for me to look good early on, I had to spend the summer doing exercises. This way I'd report to camp ready to play.

So we went to Queen Elizabeth Park in the Soo. And every day I ran, then did exercises. It wasn't all that simple, though. To help my coordination Angelo had me running backwards as well. Toward the end of the summer we rented ice and I worked on my stickhandling, my fakes, and my falling. A youngster who can stickhandle and make the puck do tricks has the edge over those boys in a junior camp who are just intent on scoring. How I'd look was the important thing.

I guess I didn't look too good. I flunked my tryout with the Tepees. There was no Junior A for me just yet. I was philosophical about it, though. I figured that I could still make it if I tried. And Angelo thought so, too. The Black Hawks wanted to farm me to their Junior B club, the Sarnia Legionairres. If I looked good there, then I'd get another crack at Junior A. My father didn't see it that way. He didn't mind the idea of my leaving home to play A hockey. At least he knew I'd be on my way. But Junior B was something else. "If you're not good enough to play Junior A, then why don't you just come home and forget about it?" he said. We had long talks, Dad, Angelo, and I; and eventually Angelo convinced my father that I should go to Sarnia. He explained that the way up wasn't easy. But if I didn't take this chance to go to Junior B, I might as well forget about the pros. Dad relented, although he still wasn't crazy about my leaving home to chase a will-o-the-wisp. By Christmas, I was the leading scorer in the league. As an amateur, I was getting $27.50 a week. How do you explain that? It's really quite simple. I was an amateur because I was called an amateur.

When you got into the juniors, it was time for most players to sign what was known as a C-Form. This provided a binding contract to the big-league club. You signed it at 18 or 19 for about a thousand dollars. It meant you were theirs. But most kids didn't think about the future. They thought about the one grand. Who thinks about his future when he's 18? The thousand is probably more money than the kid's ever seen. He could become the greatest sensation in hockey, but he's stuck with one thousand dollars. If he turns in outstanding years as a junior it doesn't matter. Luckily, I had Angelo Bombacco. He never permitted any of his players to sign with the big-league team until the kid finished with juniors. The Soos' teams were sponsored by the Chicago Black Hawks. Once

I made the Contractors I couldn't have switched even if I had wanted to. That was okay with me. I grew up a Hawks' fan. But what about other kids who wanted to go with Toronto or Montreal? Not a prayer. One of my friends was Gene Ubriaco. He wanted to play for St. Michael's, which was under Maple Leafs' sponsorship. The Hawks said no. Gene was on the Hawks' sponsored list.

When I got to be good, and thinking about turning pro, I began to hear stories about salaries and bonuses. You'd hear guys were getting money under the table as juniors, or their parents would get money so the kids would sign. That was a pretty good system for the clubs. Take a kid's old man out, buy him dinner, get him a car or give him a few thousand, and he signs away his kid's career for what seems like a good buck at the time. Beautiful. Simply beautiful.

I heard that Bobby Hull's folks got a house. I heard Roger Crozier, a heck of a goaltender, was getting 200 bucks a week while he was a junior. I don't know if the stories are true. The point is, everyone believed this went on. And where there's smoke there's fire. I never asked my dad whether he got anything. Though I suspect he did.

You'd think that of the thousands of kids tied up for life when they were just teen-agers some would have revolted when they reached legal age, some would have said, "Wait a minute. I signed this C-Form when I was under 18. This contract isn't binding." But as far as I know, no one ever did. Funny, I heard recently that Clarence Campbell, the NHL's president, said those contracts would have never stood up in court if anyone had contested them. The thing is, even if the contracts weren't valid, where could a kid go? The other clubs would have banded together against him. Just like they did with Gene Ubriaco. The teams would have had some excuse for not taking a kid who was someone else's property.

There were abuses under the system, no doubt about it. As for me, I was happy. It's only lately I've started to think, "What would have happened if I hadn't wanted to play with the Hawks?" I still don't know the answer. Maybe I wouldn't be up here today.

I mentioned I was getting $27.50 for Junior B. This included room and board. Ten dollars went for spending money. Room and board? Yes, I was at Sarnia, about 350 miles from the Soo. I was 16 or 17. Americans are always dumbfounded when you tell them hockey players at that age are living away from home. But that was the way you made it if you didn't have a real quality junior club in your home town. If you're going to improve in hockey, you have to play against better and better competition.

None of us thought it was a big deal, this business of leaving home. The arrangements for my room and board were made by Sarnia's general manager, a fellow named Tommy Norris. He set me up in a rooming house run by a lady we called Ma Dagg. There were two of us, my left wing, Richard Lachowich, and myself.

She was a terrific old lady. I know she got paid by the club, but she really took an interest. She'd wake us up at 8 in the morning, give us a good breakfast, and send us

off to school by 9. We'd come home for lunch, then back
to school till 4 o'clock. I'd return home, do some studying,
and then practice at night, maybe from 6:30 to 8.

She had been doing this sort of thing for years, and she
must have played mother to dozens of players over the
seasons. But she cared what we did, and she spent time
with us. Ma Dagg had a son, in his 30's I'd guess, and we
all played lots of cribbage together.

Still, whenever we had the chance we'd high-tail it back
to the Soo. Three or four of us on Sarnia came from the
Soo and one of the guys had a '56 Ford. We'd leave Friday
night after school, take turns at the wheel, and reach the
Soo by Saturday morning.

There's only 20 million people in Canada, and I guess a
fourth of them are clustered around Montreal, Toronto,
and Vancouver. There wasn't always a good Junior A or
B team near your home. So we had to leave, and the kids
and parents accepted this. In some ways hockey hasn't
changed much in Canada. The good players still leave
home when they're young, unless they're lucky enough to
live near a large city.

The guys I palled around with didn't mind. I think we
all saw Sarnia as a steppingstone to the big jump to the
NHL. I remember driving a truck one summer. I enjoyed
the work, but one day I was tooling around and it suddenly hit me: "God. If I don't make it in hockey I might
be doing this for the rest of my life."

It wasn't that truck-driving was demeaning. I came
from a family of workers and hard work never bothered

me. But I always thought I'd be the best at whatever I did, and that I could go as far as I really wanted to. My father worked for the Algoma Contractors. The company dealt in slag and scrap recovery—the residue left around steel mills. He started as a welder, then became a foreman.

My first job at the mills was as a water boy—I "watered the pots." Actually, they weren't pots but big pieces of steel. They had to be wet down to remove the lime dust, so the workers wouldn't inhale the stuff. I got $10 a day. But soon I wanted to drive a truck. I picked a beauty—a 40-ton diesel job called a "Euclid." The tires were as tall as I was. I also drove a Caterpillar. These we called "P.R.'s." They bounced like crazy. We took them over every damn bump in the Soo. After 10 or 15 minutes I'd have to stop to relieve myself, my body took such a pounding. It was a dump truck. The big shovel would load us up and then we'd take it over to the plant for separating.

There was another big one. This job had nine forward gears. We'd haul slag in it for three miles, and really smoke it all the way. Some of the older guys didn't like that. They figured we were making them look slow. But finally the safety supervisor got on me and we took it easy.

It was a good thing I could play. At Sarnia, all the players attended high school—or were supposed to. That was part of the system. Though you were far from home and on your own, you still had to stay in school. But I was a big shot, grabbing the 10 bucks a week, also getting some money from my dad back home. What good would high school do me? If I made it in hockey, then the education wouldn't matter. And if I didn't make it in hockey, I'd be driving a truck. High school, I thought, was a waste of time. So I quit.

Somehow, I don't think anyone in Chicago cared that a kid named Esposito, who was playing for their Junior B team in Sarnia, quit high school. I still played for them, since the school wasn't connected to the team.

My father was furious when he discovered I'd quit. He and Angelo came down from the Soo to see me. Dad had always hoped I'd go to college. He told me he had a scholarship pretty well arranged for me either at Michigan Tech (where Tony wound up) or Minnesota. I was then in my final year of high school, but I wouldn't change my mind. I tried to explain to him that it was just too hard playing hockey and going to school, that I couldn't concentrate on my schoolwork and, anyway, what did I need a diploma for? Angelo could see that I was pretty determined. "You might as well let Phil do what he wants," he told my father. Dad was so angry that he threatened to pull me out of Sarnia. I think he was hurt because I'd never told him I'd just dropped out.

Pat Esposito, my father, was a self-made man. He came up the hard way. At the age of 12, when most boys in the Soo were playing hockey, he went to work. At 15 he was working freighters on the Great Lakes after lying about his age. He was always big and he looked older. When he was ready to marry he took $2500, which had taken him five years to accumulate, and bought a two-bedroom house.

First I came along and then Tony was born. Dad didn't always have time to play with us. He was holding down two jobs—his own at the Contractors and part-time as a welder. However, he always made sure that we had someplace to play. He would flood the back yard until a sheet of ice, about 20 by 30 feet, had formed and then he'd send Tony and me out to play on it. He built a net for Tony, who was always interested in playing goal. Sometimes, though, Tony wanted to shoot the puck; so we'd call on Mother. She didn't skate, but she'd go in the nets and try to stop Tony and me. Neither Mom or Dad ever pushed us. It was more like encouragement—if we wanted to play, that was fine, and they'd do what they could to help. I know they wanted us both to go to college, something they never had. Dad also had two other obsessions: he wouldn't stand for lying or stealing. Once when I was 13 I took his Ford pick-up truck for a joy ride. I knew a little about driving, and Tony and I went for a spin. Well, somehow my father found us and we really got belted all the way home.

The biggest hurdle after Junior B is the Junior A ranks. Unless you're going to college, you've got to make Junior A to hit the big-time. The going rate in 1961 for the Junior A amateurs was $57.50 a week—plus room and board. My club was the St. Catherine Black Hawks. It was the top junior outfit in the Hawks' chain and had some quality players—Crozier, Dennis Hull, Fred Stanfield, Ken Hodge. I felt like a real big shot. I had a part-time job as a janitor, and I knew how to avoid doing the work. Richard was my roommate again. And we caused a few problems. I had my own car and we'd make it across the border to New York where you didn't have to be 21 to drink. I don't remember the name of the lady whose house we stayed in that year, but I do remember she waited up lots of nights for us to come home.

The coach was Ken Campbell. Ken's aim in life was to produce players for the Hawks. The Hawks paid his salary; we certainly didn't. Everyone else knew him as a sort of raconteur, in demand at banquets and such. To us, though, Ken was simply an extension of Chicago management. He was the closest we got to the big-time. It was a terrific team, and they could afford to do without me. In fact, that Christmas they loaned me out for a few games and I got my first taste of pro hockey. I played for the Soo Thunderbirds and for each game I received $100. Then I was back as an amateur, theoretically having received nothing.

This was another strange thing about hockey compared to other sports. They took away Jim Thorpe's medals after he won all those Olympic events because they found out he'd been a semi-pro baseball player. But in hockey you can play six pro games in any one year, get paid for them, and still be an amateur. In fact, there are some guys who've played hundreds of games—like Carl Brewer—but who then sit out a year and get back their amateur standing. Oh well, there are too many important things to worry about without trying to figure out the logic of that one.

There were lots of guys like myself who played a few games for a pro team, then went back to the amateurs. This particular Christmas, I figured I'd get my big chance. The Soos of the Eastern Professional Hockey League were hurting and they needed a center. I thought the Hawks would assign me to the Soo, turn me pro, and I'd be on my way. That's not the way it happened. I went to the Soo. I played three games. Then St. Catherines called me back. My route was stalled.

I got an inkling at the end of the season of what it's like to be thought of as property. In all sports there are managers and coaches who really don't give a damn about the player. As long as the guy performs, he's useful. Some management people don't worry about injuries either, and will let a guy play even though he may jeopardize his future. Personally, I haven't been a victim of this. I've usually found my coaches to be pretty understanding about injuries. In fact, the really good coaches insist that injuries be reported. They know you're no good to the club if you hurt. But you've got to look out for yourself. Don't trust anyone else to do it.

Once St. Catherines was in the first round of Memorial Cup competition. The Memorial Cup is Canada's top junior prize, like the Stanley Cup is for the NHL. In the first game of Cup play, I broke my wrist. Naturally, I was finished—or so I thought. I was wiped out of Memorial Cup play. But the Soo Thunderbirds were still playing their Eastern League season. They had three games remaining, and ironically, three games were how many I had left of eligibility. Bob Wilson, the Hawks' chief scout, thought I might play for the Soo, however. So Wilson asked me if I wanted to finish out the season with the Thunderbirds. Here I was with a broken wrist keeping me out of amateur competition, and a man from the Chicago Black Hawks was asking me if I wanted to play three games in the pros.

I didn't know what to do. When you're a kid you can't make an intelligent decision on something like this. I was just wondering how effective I'd be. I never even thought about the injury endangering my career if I played—maybe even crippling me. I asked Dad and he was against it. I asked the family doctor, and he said not to, that it could finish me as a hockey player. Everyone was against it. Me, I wasn't so sure. Finally, I spoke to Wilson. I told him I didn't know what would happen to the wrist if I played. He said—and I'll never forget it—"If you want to play, then play. If you're worried about the wrist, then don't."

That's a terrific piece of advice. I mean, I really knew about bones and all, right? I could really make the decision, right? Of course, I did the dumb thing. All I could think about was that here was another chance to show off before the fans in my home town. I decided to play. You know the size of the cast they put on someone's broken wrist? Well, it's pretty big. You'd never get a glove over it. And you're not allowed to play unless you wear a glove. Anyway, I couldn't play with that big thing on. So I went down to the basement and found a file. Then I hid behind the furnace, because I didn't want Dad to see what I was doing. I was sweating like a son of a gun, and scared too, as I began to cut the cast down. I was huffing and puffing, working to file the damn thing so thin that I could wrap my hand around a stick. As I filed, I kept thinking: "I've got to make this thing work. I don't want to wind up driving a truck for the steel mill. I've got to be a pro."

I played, and it almost cost me a career. That summer the wrist simply refused to heal. It hurt constantly. I think I made half a dozen trips to the doctor who manipulated the cast every which way. The bones refused to knit properly. Somehow, they eventually did and I remember the doctor telling me how "lucky" I was. Luck. Isn't that something? That a kid's career should hinge on luck? Wasn't there someone around the team, someone maybe with the Chicago organization, who could have told me: don't do it. You've still got a job with us. You don't have to show off for our sake. That's not the way it was, though. I was worried. I saw the chance to play three games in the pros— and I was afraid of losing it.

So luck was with me. I think about luck and hockey quite a bit, especially when I'm asked about scoring 70 goals or getting 150 points. I've simply been a big lucky stiff through most of my pro career. Whenever I'm asked about scoring records, the first thing that comes to mind is avoiding injuries. Every player thinks about it. In February of the 1971–72 season I was 1 point ahead of the Rangers' Jean Ratelle, a truly fine guy. At one of the Ranger workouts a fan came up to Jean and said, "Well, you've got 46 goals now—a few more games and you'll get your 50." Ratty replied, "You never know what'll happen." So the next night Jean broke his ankle and was finished for the season.

I think more and more about injuries. I remember Jim Krulicki, a good little player who came up in the Rangers' organization and then was traded to Detroit. He quit hockey while he was still in his early 20's. He said that the people in the game didn't care about the player, only what he could produce. Krulicki had an experience similar to mine. Only his was his knee. When he was in juniors, he played with a bad knee after the team doctors told him it would be okay. Later Krulicki found out that he had been fooling around with a potential crippling injury. "When I got to the NHL," Krulicki said, "the doctors told me I never should have played with my knee in that condition."

2

Chicago and Billy Reay

My career wasn't over. In a sense it was just starting. I was ready to turn pro, but not quite ready for that supreme bit of aggravation known as Signing Your First Pro Contract. You've got to understand this about athletes: we're athletes. We're not businessmen. If you're a truck driver, what do you know about contracts? Probably nothing. If you're a ballet dancer about to begin a professional career, what do you know about money and taxes? Not too much. But athletes are expected to sign with a team and intelligently evaluate how much they're worth when they've never even been exposed to significant money before. And when I was coming up, you did it yourself. No business advisor, no agent.

I didn't have much going for me when I reported to the Chicago training camp in the fall of 1962. The hand had murdered me during the summer. I was overweight from inaction. I was slow. I couldn't show them much in camp.

And I was nervous as hell. What position was I in to talk contract?

So there I was, standing in a hallway of the Queensway Hotel in St. Catherines—me and a bunch of other rookies waiting to talk to Tommy Ivan, the general manager of the Chicago Black Hawks.

I had met Ivan once before, when he presented me with a trophy in a kids' league back home. He handed me the award and said, "You're a big one." Now it was five years later, and I was waiting my turn to go in and talk money with him. I'll tell you, waiting with a bunch of guys, some of them farmers with white socks and brown shoes, doesn't get you in a real tough frame of mind. The feeling you have is fear, and it spreads down the line. It's almost as if the Hawks had planned this scene, like in an Army induction center: okay, you're next, bend down and touch your toes. When you walk into that room with the general manager—from Chicago, of all places—you've been depersonalized. "My, you're a big one," he had said to me. I wondered if he'd remember that as I pulled myself together to discuss money with him.

You always hear the guys talking. "Hey, what are you going to ask for? How much did so-and-so get?" There's a grapevine in camp, and you get a pretty good idea of what the salaries are. Even though I'd never been a professional (the money in juniors was amateur money, of course) I had a few figures in mind for what I thought was a fair salary. But I was soon to learn something about contracts and salary.

I don't know what it is—or was—about Tommy Ivan. That man has always scared me to death. Perhaps it was because my whole future was in his hands. If he didn't want me, I was through. Maybe it's his sophistication. He's a good-looking man, with distinguished gray hair. And he dresses beautifully. He could sleep in his suit and the crease in his trousers would still be sharp the next morning. Everything about him is carefully planned. And me, sometime truck driver, I was going to talk contract with this man.

It wasn't quite as simple as I thought. I learned about three-way contracts. I learned about different bonus arrangements, depending on what league you wound up with. Ivan asked me what I wanted. I told him that it would cost him a $2500 bonus to get me to sign to play with the Black Hawks. And in salary I wanted $10,000 for the big leagues. But I knew I might not make it in the NHL, so I told Ivan I wanted $2000 as a bonus and $6500 for the season in case I was assigned to the American League. For the Eastern Pro League, I was downright modest. One thousand bucks as a bonus, and $5000 for the season would get me to play there.

Nothing happened.

I wasn't exactly asking for the world. But Ivan seemed shocked at my demands. I kept working out in camp, and I was fat and slow. We talked several more times. It was getting obvious that I wasn't going to jump to the NHL just yet. The Eastern Pro League was where they had me ticketed. Now, all we had to do was agree on price. I didn't think my demand was so outrageous: $1000 as a bonus to get the Black Hawks to sign me for life. And $5000 for a season. That was a fair enough wage. In 1962 the average blue-collar worker was earning that much.

After a few weeks Gus Kyle, the Soos' coach, came over to me.

"They're offering you $500 to sign and $3250 for the season," he said. "You'd better take it. That's all Mr. Ivan says you'll get." Then Kyle threw in the clincher: "If you don't sign, you can't play anywhere."

Of course he was right! And I knew it. But I didn't stop to realize that if they really thought I could cut it, they wouldn't drop me or let me go back home to stew about it. They wanted me playing. Anyway, I was ready to sign. However, I got a bit more than Kyle had mentioned. I got the thousand bonus, and a fat $3800 for the year.

I was in the fold. It was their job to bluff me—and they did. I wonder now what would have happened if I had called their bluff. I'm sure they'd have signed me for what I wanted, or close to it. But I'm philosophical about it now. After all, it wasn't their fault I was ignorant.

But was I ever scared at the time that I'd be buried. That's the term we use. When a club is fed up with a player it buries him in its minor league system. Give them a hard time and they've got all the edges. The Hawks tried to bluff Ray Cullen, a pretty good hockey player. He wouldn't sign and they told him they'd bury him. Instead, he went to Knoxville and remained an amateur. He spit in their faces. They came around to him eventually. This happened at the same time I was going through my contract difficulties. Cullen had the guts to stick it out; I didn't. Sure enough, the next year he signed for what he had wanted—the bonus, the salary. He knew he was good. I did too. But could I really buck the whole Black Hawks' organization? No. I wasn't that sure.

You see, before expansion they could really bury a guy. There was a fellow named Murray Balfour who held out for a lot of money. The way I heard it, Ivan finally came around to Balfour's terms telling him: "I'll pay you—but I'll bury you." Ubriaco was another guy like that. He was a big scorer in the minors but he couldn't make it in Chicago. He could have made it someplace else if they had traded him, though. Except that would have strengthened another team, and the Hawks didn't want that. Guys like Ubriaco weren't traded; they just waited in the minors. Another one was Matt Ravlich. He knocked around the minors for years. He could have played in the big leagues.

Ubriaco finally quit in 1971. He was a victim of what is known as "waivers." Waivers are supposed to protect a player's rights. It works like this: any player who's been a pro at least three years and has appeared in at least six games cannot be assigned to the minors unless every other team in the league gets a chance to buy him for the waiver price. Supposedly this gives a player a chance to remain in the NHL. Somehow, the Hawks got waivers from the 13 other clubs. That meant they weren't interested, and Ubriaco still remained Chicago property. But we players know that owners often cook up deals among themselves—

you leave my guy alone, and I'll do you a favor some time. That's what happened with Gene, I'm sure. The Hawks assigned him to Portland—at an $8000 salary cut. He quit. Gene had some pride left.

Another way the rules are sidestepped is in this business of protecting players in the draft. When the first expansion draft was held in 1967, the original teams were allowed to protect a certain number of players on their roster. Everyone else was fair game (or supposed to be). The catch was this: any player not taken on the first round could then be protected. Fair enough. But the Canadiens, for example, left Claude Provost unprotected. Now, there's just no way an expansion team would fail to pick up Provost. He's one of the smartest little players around. Yet, he wasn't taken, and the Canadiens quickly removed him from the unprotected list. You can't tell me nobody wanted Claude Provost. Ridiculous. The rules say it's supposed to be an open draft. No deals. Everyone knows there must have been other considerations for the teams that left Provost alone.

That was all way ahead back in 1962, my first season as a pro. My salary didn't go far, even in those days. When the season was over I owed $1200 to some guy who killed me at poker. We were just a bunch of kids far from home. No one told us how to manage our money. No one was thinking about his future. It's probably still like that in the low minors. But today's kids have more money than we did. When I turned pro, the usual bonus was $1000. Now it's about $10,000, and some youngsters like Gil Perreault or Guy Lafleur probably got $35,000. Why not? Just because a club drafts you and has the rights to negotiate with you, doesn't mean they shouldn't pay something to get you to play with them.

My first season up was really something. Actually, I came to roost in St. Louis where the Soos' team had been shifted. We were a bunch of wild bachelors, and Gus Kyle used to call us the Chinese Bandits. We'd sleep all day, gamble at night. We were interested in freedom, not saving money. Still, that was a good year for me. I had 90 points in 71 games, and scored 35 goals. When you're young you can get away with a little easy living. I wonder what some coaches would say about those 90 points, combined with my life-style? No doubt a few would comment that I'd have done even better if I had been a good boy. But as far as I'm concerned, being a good hockey player isn't really a bed by 9 and up at 6 thing.

All this had one disastrous effect, though. I was broke. I had to put off my wedding scheduled for June. So instead of happily settling down with Linda after the season, I got a job driving trucks again, and took home $90 a week. I saved every penny, and we got married in August. It was a good thing for me that at Italian weddings everyone gives you cash. I needed the bread. But of course I blew it on a Bel Air convertible and a honeymoon in Florida.

Lots of people think we're above manual labor, that once we put on a uniform we're suddenly on a different plateau. I never felt that way. Even when I made it with the Hawks I continued to drive a truck in the summer;

in fact, I did this every summer until I got traded to Boston. I had to. I certainly couldn't live on what the Hawks were paying me. Some found that hard to believe. Guys would come up to me and say, "Why are you driving a truck. Don't players make $50,000 a year?" Luckily, I enjoyed truck driving.

My second season playing for pay was about to begin, and I figured I'd really learned the ropes. No more monkeying around with Ivan. I'd had a good season. They had to listen to me. St. Louis was now in the Central League as the old Eastern Pro League lost its name. But I found that nothing had really changed. I wanted a one-way contract of $6500, no matter where I played. Remember, I'd only asked for $5000 the year before as a rookie to play for St. Louis. I had 90 points. Was $6500 asking too much? According to Ivan it was. He offered me $4500. A $700 raise over what he had paid an untried rookie! Why players don't blow their stacks when an offer like that comes along I'll never know. Doesn't the general manager think we've got pride? Yet, strangely I suppose, I don't blame the guy. His job is to get every player as cheap as possible. If I were in his shoes I'd have tried the same thing. Finally, we compromised. But only after I learned a lot about bonus clauses and figured I was in pretty good shape to pick up this extra money—you know, for reaching certain figures. So I signed for $5500, plus the bonus clauses.

At first glance this bonus business looks like a pretty

good thing for us. But when you stop to think about it, it actually works out in management's favor. True, bonus money can really add up. At St. Louis it could have come to as much as $2500 for me—which would work out to $8000 for the season. There was a bonus if I made the All-Star team, a bonus for getting 20 goals, then 25 goals, then 30 goals. Things like that. Well, I had a pretty good first year and I figured there'd be no problem earning the bonus money.

But hold on a second. What if a guy doesn't reach the bonus figures? Say he gets injured. Then the club only has to pay him his salary. And if you do reach the bonus money, then you're perhaps only getting what you deserve to be paid anyway. In other words, management still has the edge. They can't get hurt.

I was right about earning my bonus money. After half a season I'd already earned most of it. So my pay for the year would be $8000. Not bad. But then on January 16, 1964, the Hawks called me up. And you know what happened—I was put under a major league contract, for the minimum of $7500 a season. I was taking a cut in pay!

They didn't say a word about the bonus money. I was losing it and they never even offered to make up the difference. But perhaps I was a dope not to just ask for it. As it was, I didn't say a thing. And maybe they figured I was going to share in the playoff money anyway. Maybe. But I have the nagging feeling they just didn't care. The playoff money shouldn't have had anything to do with it, however, because it didn't cost the Hawks anything. That's an automatic bonus paid by the league.

Of course, I wasn't thinking about the $500 difference as I took my first plane ride to join the Hawks. The first time any kid's on his way to the big leagues he's not thinking about money. Instead I thought to myself, "Wow! I'm going to meet Bobby Hull." I was too nervous to eat on the flight. And when I got to the Montreal Forum two hours before game-time Billy Reay, the Hawks' coach, recognized the symptoms.

I think I would have thrown up if I'd eaten that day. I couldn't look at food. I felt a little better when Reay sent me in to see Nick Garen, the Hawks' trainer. He pulled out a uniform for me. It had belonged to Murray Hall, who was sent down to St. Louis when I was called up. I was happy with the uniform—it was Number 7, the same number I'd worn all through the kids' league. I felt it brought me luck. A few years later, when I was traded to the Bruins, I got the same number again. One of the Boston players in the deal was Pit Martin. Martin had worn Number 7, and I got it.

I put on my uniform and sat down next to Chico Maki, who was nice enough to say, "Hi, Phil, how are you?" Bobby Hull also came over to shake hands. Just then I heard someone shout, "Hey, we got a wop aboard now."

I'd arrived.

When I took the ice for the pre-game warm-up, I felt like a big shot, skating in circles near Hull, taking shots at Glenn Hall. And I even had an ear open to the fans in the stands, because I remember one voice asking: "Who's Number 7? That's not Murray Hall."

No matter how great a fellow is in the minors, he's scared—not just nervous—when he takes his first shift on the ice. That night I played two shifts, about three minutes. And that was it. In the next few games I saw little action. Reay didn't tell me much, only to watch his centers and learn.

So I became a bench-warmer. You always hear bench-warmers say, "I'm where I am for the good of the team." Or "the coach knows what he's doing." Don't believe it. There isn't one guy sitting on the bench in Oakland or Montreal or Detroit who doesn't feel he's better than someone else out on the ice. That's the way it was with me. The thrill of just making it quickly wore off. Soon, I was watching the other guys and thinking to myself that I could do the job better than this one or that one. You have to think that way or else your pride goes down the drain. But for the public and the press, we go along with the coach and sit on the bench "for the good of the team."

I was getting bitchy not playing, while guys who weren't half as good skated regularly. Some games I suited up and spent 60 minutes on the bench. Other times I'd go in for a shift or two. When you play under conditions like that, you try to beat the whole damn world in those 90 seconds on the ice. You figure that if you mess up you won't get another chance. And you know something—you don't. When people talk about a rookie pressing, it's real. That pressure is so heavy you feel it on your shoulders. A big

guy like me, I needed time to unwind. But no sooner did
I get on the ice than, yank, I was back on the bench, without even working up a sweat.

That's why it's so easy for a rookie or a mediocre player
to look bad. When you press you're not playing intelligently. The guys know that. Yet they feel this is their one
chance all night, and wind up playing stupidly. How can
you tell a fellow who's worried about being shipped down
to the minors to just take it easy, play your game, don't
get excited. Sure, you can tell him. But he won't listen.
Every year half a dozen hot-shot rookies come up. Big
things are expected. But they don't produce and get
traded. What happens? They blossom. The pressure's off;
they're looked upon as losers and anything they do is
like a bonus. So they play their game and forget about
having to impress the fans or their coach. If you're good,
it'll show eventually.

Meanwhile, I learned my wife Linda was pregnant.
She was still back in St. Louis, all alone. It suddenly hit
me—I was just another body to Chicago. They weren't
playing me, and they didn't care. If you wanted attention,
you had to scream.

Which is what I did. "What the hell am I doing here?"
I asked Reay. "My wife's back in St. Louis, alone and
pregnant. I'm here sitting on the bench. I'd rather be back
in St. Louis."

One thing about Tommy Ivan. He likes family. Maybe
he's like other hockey executives in that respect. He figures you get into less trouble if you've got a wife and

kids around. Reay told Ivan I was screaming, and Tommy brought my wife to Chicago. That didn't change my playing situation any. I was still a bench-warmer, only now Linda was there to share my misery. I still didn't have an inkling what the future held, and the way they were using me I was becoming more disillusioned and uncertain. Maybe this will give you an idea of the absurd situation I was in, and the pressures I was feeling.

Ivan, big on family, invited my folks and Linda and me to dinner near his home in Skokie. As we drove to the restaurant, I kept pressuring Dad to ask Ivan about me, whether I'd make the team. I had been up for over a month, yet I'd been afraid to question him myself. I don't know if it was because I was young or unsure but I dreaded asking Ivan anything. I suppose I wasn't really so different from other rookies who go through their first season afraid to ask about themselves, afraid they'll give management ideas that perhaps they're troublemakers or wise guys. So me, big shot pro hockey player, I ask Dad to talk to the boss. There I was, sitting at the table, kicking my father's feet so he would ask Ivan. Then they started to talk about me as though I weren't even there, a kid sitting in the corner while the teacher talks about the bright future of her pupil to the child's parents. It was an awful dinner. But Ivan assured Dad I'd be given a chance.

We sat at a big table. I was on one end, Tommy was on the other. The waiter came around for the drink order, but I was afraid that would be breaking training. I was on my best behavior. Boy, was that strange. I looked at everyone having a drink, and then everyone putting butter on his bread—and I just sat there. I didn't even want to eat the bread. Of course, I ate a steak. I didn't have to change my routine for that. Steak is practically the only thing I order in a restaurant.

Somehow, I lasted the season. I appeared (or sat through) 27 games, a figure I didn't much think about at the time. But later, those 27 games would teach me another lesson. As the playoffs approached, the regular season didn't bother me any more. I was hoping to get into Stanley Cup play. Then I did something I'll never forgive myself for.

Our opponent in the first playoff round was the Detroit Red Wings. It went to seven games. I had played in four of them, and knew I wouldn't be seeing any action in the final one at Chicago. Normally, I'd sit in the press box. That's the favorite place for players who are benched. But I was so angry at the way things had gone that I told Linda we were clearing out fast. I had a feeling we'd lose the final game, and why the hell did they need me just to watch from the press box? Win or lose, though (and we lost), I should have been there. Yet bright and early the next morning, we piled into our already packed car and set off for the Soo.

There was another bad thing about that playoff. The rap started about me being a lousy playoff performer. The record books show that I was in four games and didn't even get one point. What the books don't show is that I was up for a cup of coffee. I didn't see much action. But

it's there in black and white. I wonder how much worse
the rap would have been if people knew that I'd cleared
out of town, not even waiting to console my teammates.

I went through hell for my contract the next year. Once
again, it showed me how they sucker a young player. Many
of us sign for two years or three years when we first come
up. We're afraid we may not make it, and we want that
guaranteed income. It's a sucker bet. I wanted $15,000
and a one-way contract. So even if they sent me back to
the minors they'd still pay me the $15,000. Ivan, of course,
didn't exactly agree. He wanted a three-way contract, with
three different salaries. Eventually I signed a two-way
contract, for two years. It was worth $10,500 the first year
and $12,500 the second. It doesn't sound so big when you
say it that way. But when the general manager discusses
it, he says, "We're giving you a $23,000 contract for two
years." That sounds a lot better. Often you read about a
player's signing, say, a $200,000 contract for three years.
He's not getting 200 G's every year. It's spread over three
years. But the public and the press usually gloss right
over that. They just see the big figure and assume that's
the man's salary.

My two-year deal took a lot out of me. I didn't want it,
but Ivan talked me into it. He said, "Phil, you've got security. You'll get $23,000 for two years, no matter what
happens." He didn't add, "even if you get 50 goals." Boy,
do they know when they've got a sucker on the line. Looking back, I realize there was absolutely no advantage for
me in signing for the two years. In the first place, I wasn't
making that much above the minimum. If I had a bad

year, how much could they cut me? But if I had a really good one, I could have demanded a lot more the second year.

There's another thing about signing a contract. They tell all the guys not to talk around, that "it's between us." Well, that's to keep you ignorant. If you start talking maybe you'll find out there's guys not half as good as you are getting more money. But when the general manager says "it's between us," you start thinking, hell, I'd better not spoil a good thing.

Well, they got their $10,500 worth. I had a good season. In fact, I began thinking about rookie-of-the-year honors. And then I found out I was ineligible. I had played (hah!) in 27 games the previous season. To be considered a rookie you couldn't appear in more than 25 games in any previous year. Brother, was I ticked off. I just couldn't believe it. But if you take one turn on the ice, it counts as a game played. I must have had 10 games like that, where all I did was step on the ice and step off. Neither Reay nor Ivan ever mentioned the 25 games to me. Maybe it was my fault, because I'm sure Reay never thought of it. Still, you know, I'll bet that even if I'd said something to him he would have dressed me. Billy wouldn't give a player an inch. I've heard he's changed. But in those days management had absolute power. You didn't question a thing. Anyway I scored 23 goals and added 32 assists for 55 points. Not bad for a rookie. Roger Crozier captured the award. I don't say I'd have taken it, but I would've given it a hell of a shot. The award was worth $1000.

I began my second full season a proven 20-goal scorer—and was making $12,500. Who do you think got the better of my two-year "guaranteed security?" The Hawks were pretty secure, I'll tell you. During that rookie season of 1964–65, only 23 players scored 20 or more goals. I was one of them. And I'm sure I was the only one getting $12,500 the next year. The Hawks never offered me a new contract. To tell the truth, at the time I didn't think they should have. I figured I'd made a deal and signed my name to it. They certainly didn't owe me more money legally. But what about morally?

One thing I knew—I was going to get the jump on them next time. My goal production went up to 27 during the 1965–66 campaign, not bad for a $200-a-week player. Midway along, I began thinking about the following year's contract. It was going to be a big one, I decided. I still thought I could do all the talking myself. Of course, if there'd been a history of players bringing lawyers along to talk contract at that time, I'd have had one too. But you always wind up doing what others have done. And I was no different.

But just about that time the league began talking expansion. Good players would suddenly be worth more money. Even mediocre players would be worth something, because there were going to be 12 teams instead of six. Expansion would be a blessing for us. So we organized into a Players Association, with Toronto lawyer Alan Eagleson at the head.

For really the first time in NHL history, the guys were

together, and we had someone to go to for advice. I discussed my salary with Eagleson, and told him what I was going to ask for under a new contract. He told me to stand firm, that the players would back every other player who was in a contract dispute. I felt on really solid ground. I wasn't worried any more about being buried. And others felt the same way. You've got to understand that for years the owners had this little habit of trading away union organizers. As soon as any guy gave an owner too much lip, zoom, he was in the boondocks. But now I was going to get what I believed I deserved.

The trouble was, Ivan didn't believe I deserved what I was asking. We began a long series of negotiations once the season ended. He said he was being fair, that he was offering me a 25 percent raise. Which sounds a lot. One-fourth more money. But it came down to only a few thousand dollars. Sure, $3000 is a 25 percent jump when you're earning $12,500. But the $12,500 wasn't a fair starting point. I had been stuck with that salary under the two-year deal. I was worth more than $12,500 that season. The average 27-goal scorer was probably making $20,000. Why not give me a 25 percent raise on that figure?

We negotiated for so damn long that the season was about ready to start and I didn't have a contract. When that happens you go to arbitration—the one thing I didn't want. You know who the arbitrator was? Clarence Campbell, president of the league. That's a heck of a note. He's a nice guy, and he's fair. But he's paid by the owners; he never received a cent from me.

How would you like it if you were working on the assembly-line for Pontiac and you ask your boss for more money and he says no. So you go to arbitration—and the arbitrator is the president of General Motors?

In those days we played the All-Star game before the regular season began. We only had six teams, and the club that had won the Stanley Cup would be given a sort of bonus by hosting the game between the All-Stars and the Cup defender. Reay was the All-Star coach since the Hawks had made it to the final round before losing to Montreal. I was in Montreal talking to Ivan and getting nowhere. Arbitration was looming ahead. Then, a few days before the game, Reay comes over to me. Out of the blue he says, very offhandedly, "I'm thinking of using you in the All-Star game. You want to play?"

Well, hell, that's some honor. Of course I did, I told him. It never occurred to me that you can't play in the game unless you've signed your contract.

All simple me thought about was that Reay was a heck of a guy to select me. Ulterior motives? I was so excited I rushed to tell Bobby Hull and Chico Maki. I really blabbered. Soon, I was back in negotiations with Ivan about the contract. The game was coming up. I refused to sign. Ivan, giving me one of his ultimatums, said, "Well, that's it. We'll have to go to arbitration."

The next thing I knew, Reay picked Eric Nesterenko for the All-Star team.

Reay never mentioned another word to me about playing in the game. It was as though the conversation hadn't

even taken place. Suddenly it hit me, and there was no
question, he'd been using the All-Star game as a wedge to
make me sign. It blew my mind.

Despite the threats, we never went to arbitration. I
signed another two-year deal. I was to get $17,500 the
first year and $20,000 the second. It was quite a season.
For the first time in history, the Hawks finished first. I had
21 goals, but a fat zero in six playoff games as we got
knocked out in the opening round. I knew that Reay
wasn't impressed with me as a playoff performer. Still, in
three seasons with Chicago I had scored 23, 27, and 21
goals. So what happened? I was traded to Boston. A last-
place club.

For the first time in my hockey life, I had been rejected.
Guys talk about trades being part of the game. I suppose
it's always in the back of your mind if you're a professional athlete. But when it happens—pow. It's a slap in
the face. What it means to a guy is that someone doesn't
think enough of him to keep him around. That was my
reaction anyway. Maybe if you go from a bad club to a
winner you're thrilled. But Boston? That was a last-place
team. They hadn't been in the playoffs since 1959. It was
like the guys on the Hawks were consoling me at a wake.
"You'll like it in Boston," they said. "It's a great hockey
town." That wasn't my reaction, though. There was shame.
I had scored 71 goals in three years, and my club thought
they were getting someone better. Funny, isn't it, that the
first thing you ask when you're told you've been traded is:
"Who did they trade me for?" Then when you find out the

guy's name, you try to rationalize that he's really pretty good, maybe even a bigger name than you are. Every guy I know who's ever been traded wants to know: "Who'd they get for me?"

Yet, there was something positive about the Boston deal. For the first time I realized I was a celebrity. I never thought people knew my name or that the papers cared much about me. But when the trade was announced, I was the major figure in the deal. The Hawks had to get rid of me before I saw my name in big type. At Chicago I'd been overshadowed by Bobby Hull, Stan Mikita, Glenn Hall, Ken Wharram. All of a sudden, I was a big man in Boston. Together with Orr. And I liked that.

I also liked dealing with the Bruins. I was in the second year of my Hawks' contract, which Boston took over. They didn't have to give me more than the $20,000 the contract called for. But one of the inducements to sign with a con-tender—sign, that is, for a bit less than you think you really deserve—is that you're practically guaranteed playoff money. So a $20,000 contract with a club that will finish in the top four was actually worth $21,500 at least. Even if you lose the first round of Stanley Cup play, you receive $1500 a man. I had a long talk with Milt Schmidt, the Bruins' general manager. I told him that his guys hadn't been in the playoffs for years, while I had and should be compensated for that. The Bruins, after all, were not likely to make the playoffs, and I was accustomed to getting that extra money. There's also something else. When you come from a first-place club to a last-place club you bring a winning attitude—and that can help the team. Schmidt gave me a $22,500 contract. He also made me an assistant captain, which is an honor. Especially for a new guy. It showed they respected me and valued my judgment.

It's nice to feel wanted. And in Boston I did. I'd gone through a traumatic summer after the trade, worrying as well as discussing my future with Dad. We'd sit over a beer and I'd tell him how depressed I was at leaving a first-place club to go to a last-place team. Little by little, Dad's positive attitude changed me around. "Afraid of a little work?" he'd ask. And I'd answer, "Of course not." He insisted that I was good enough to make it anywhere and that I could help the Bruins. "Just show them what you can do," he would say. By the time camp started I had stopped sulking. I'd show the Hawks and I'd show the Bruins. In fact, I'd show the whole damned hockey world who Phil Esposito was.

There's a big difference in playing for a team on which you're overshadowed and playing for another club where you really feel needed. It was that way for me in Boston. And in my second home game I scored four goals.

That night Dad called. "You see," he said. "There's nothing to it." And he was right. It turned into a really good season. I had 35 goals and the most assists in the league —49. I finished second to Mikita in scoring.

Naturally, if I knew I'd get 126 points during the 1968–69 season, I'd have asked for $100,000 per year. But no one figures to get 126 points. I mean, no one had even gotten 100 points before.

So I was quite happy with the deal I made before the 1968–69 campaign began. A three-year contract worth a total of $115,000. It went up in steps, with the final year—1970–71—worth about $41,000. Well, after that fantastic season I thought they'd jump my contract. So I told Milt Schmidt, "I know you're not legally bound to; still, isn't there a moral question here?" But the Bruins said they'd never rip up a contract. Though they were pretty fair about the whole thing. They gave me good bonuses. Yet, I couldn't wait for the contract to end.

The final year I skyrocketed. I got 152 points and 76 goals. I busted Bobby Hull's mark by 18 goals. But my salary was only $400 more than I'd been making two years before.

Then we negotiated the new contract. It took a summer to figure out all the fine points. I needed my business partner, Fred Sharf, and my lawyer, Arnold Bloom, to help set it up. I signed a four-year deal that some people believe is worth about $150,000 a year. But one writer guessed I was getting only $100,000 a year. Now that really bothers me. After all, I've got my pride.

3

The Price—and
Rewards—of Fame

After the 126-point year certain people began to appear. Where they came from I'll never know. There must be a well-trained army somewhere with a mission: get a guy whose name you see in the paper and sign him on. Suddenly I was being tugged and clawed, smothered with offers and deals, wild, bizarre, funny. The thing was, most of them would cost me money.

How does Phil Esposito's Home Decorators strike you? That was one offer. How about Phil Esposito Safaris? It became incredible. Stock deals, franchises, vending machines. Can't miss. Double your money in a year. But first . . . but first, Phil, a little good-faith money on your part. Oh, only a thou, and you get a 50 percent partnership.

Fred Sharf and I first got together in 1967, soon after

I had been traded to Boston. The way Fred tells the story I was the only hockey player (except for Bobby Hull) he'd ever heard of. How come me? Well, he was sitting at a game once and some fan screamed all night, "Esposito, you're a bum!" That's how Fred knew my name. Fred also had the same insurance man as Tom Johnson did. Tom was our personnel director then. Fred wanted to expand his sporting-goods business and figured that if he could get a pro player to endorse his hockey line and make some changes in the equipment, he could increase sales. It's a funny thing about the sporting-goods business: people will buy a player-endorsed product 5 to 1 over one that doesn't have a big name behind it. Anyway, Fred asked Tom to suggest a player; and Tom must have seen potential in me that the Black Hawks didn't. He told Fred, "We think Phil will be a great one."

By this time I had learned a little something about business. I'd been running a hockey school back home. But a line of athletic equipment was a whole new thing. First off, I wanted it to be good. There are guys in our sport who never set foot inside a factory that makes equipment with their name on it. They don't know if its crummy or not, never even tried the stuff. I saw a great future in hockey equipment. The boom was just starting in the States, and there were millions of kids who would buy hockey gear. I visited factories with Fred, and we devised new equipment or changed existing equipment to meet my standards. The first check I received was for $1000 against 5 percent royalties. By the end of the first year,

Fred's hockey sales had increased 10 times and I wound up with a $5000 royalty. The next year it was $20,000, and now it's six figures just for the products that say "Phil Esposito" on them. The line is doing more than $5-million worth of business each year, and growing.

I'm a genius, right? Not exactly. The first endorsement I ever made was for an iceless hockey puck, a forerunner of the street puck we put out today. I signed with the manufacturer, a fellow in Chicago. He offered $500 against 5 percent royalties. That $500 was all I saw. I know he sold more than $10,000 worth. But when it came time to pay me, he had financial problems. That experience taught Fred and me something—up-front money is essential.

Athletes are fair game for every quick-buck artist that comes along. There's one "agent" who's got a great con. He's signed half a dozen hockey players on the same team in an expansion city. Now, here's what he does for them. He tells the player, "Look, sign with me. I'll negotiate your contract. I take 5 percent. But I'll also get you endorsements. I get 15 percent of the endorsements, but that's fair enough—it's found money." That's a pretty good deal. Except for one thing. He never gets them the endorsements. So these poor guys are giving the agent 5 percent of their salary for absolutely nothing. You know what he made in "endorsements" for one of the team's top players? A fat $400. The next year the same fellow went on his own and made five times that.

There's another attorney who's got a sweetheart of a racket. And he really socked it to a friend of mine. This lawyer asks guys to put up $10,000 apiece. "I'm investing it in deals," he tells them. When you ask him what deals, he sort of waffles around. Well, my friend was getting a little worried. He told Fred about the money. By now he had put in more than $20,000. Fred knows something about business and called up the lawyer to ask about the money. This fellow told Fred, "Don't worry. He's getting a return on his investment." Investment in what? Fred wanted to know. The lawyer said, "It's too complicated." Still Fred had learned a few things at Harvard, so finally he demanded the player's money back. The fellow complied. He sent Fred a letter telling him that my friend had earned $2000 interest on his $20,000 investment. However, there was a legal fee of $3000. So my friend wound up losing a thousand dollars after having $20,000 sit around for three years. Actually, he got off pretty easy.

Maybe that's why I'm scared of stocks. Three times I've invested, and three times I've lost money. But I'm lucky. There are guys in hockey who've gotten burned a dozen times, and they keep going to the well. Hustlers are always coming around, especially to the big-money players. They figure you're making a good buck and don't know what to do with it. I've had offers from guys who promised to double my money in a week. Not a month—a week. Of course, I've fallen for it. Five or six of us on the Bruins each put up $1500 a few years ago. It was for stock in a Canadian gold mine, selling for 85 cents a share. For $1500 we owned more than 1000 shares of stock. That's a nice feeling. But the stock's not even quoted now.

I suppose my real education—in business, in friendship, really in living—came after the 126-point season. Fred and I had been together about a year. I'd done a few things on my own. But the skies opened after all those points. People were bugging me with propositions, and I didn't know where to start. First thing we decided to do was to form a corporation. This put me, according to Fred, "one step removed from all those people who want Phil Esposito's time." At least this way when we wanted to say no to a deal, it would come from the corporation and not from me personally. You don't make as many enemies that way.

Every man dreams of seeing his name wherever he goes and having this mean something. I'm no exception. So when I went into the hockey equipment business with Fred I was determined that whatever we sold would be as good as we could possibly make it. If it wasn't, I didn't want my name on it.

The next thing Fred and I did was to travel to Montreal and visit factories that make hockey equipment. One made protective gear—helmets, pads, gloves—and the other made sticks. We were going to put out a Phil Esposito line of equipment, from head to toe. The world of business was a completely new adventure for me and my adrenalin was flowing.

When we visited the stick factory we found that the quality of sticks they were producing for youngsters was relatively poor. Most kids, in fact, use cut-down sticks. They get a regulation stick and simply saw off the end. But it's out of balance. And the smaller sticks for sale aren't generally more than toys. I figured kids needed a real stick and we set about making one. I wanted a decent grade of handle and a fiberglass-faced blade. In short, it would be made well. The same was true for hockey gloves. First, I wanted black-and-gold colors. They look big-league and also happen to be the Bruins' colors. I made certain modifications in these as well. Soon I was designing shin guards and all sorts of protective equipment, until we had a full line of Phil Esposito products ready for market. No hockey player had ever developed a full-scale line of gear before.

Not everyone in New England jumped at the opportunity to sell the stuff. We told buyers that if they bought the line I'd make personal appearances in their stores—which I did. It was a strange sensation at first. I hate wearing suits. Yet, I thought I should wear one—after all, I was a businessman. So I dug out a double-breasted model and Fred asked me what funeral I was attending. Today I wear a turtleneck and sports jacket.

Sometimes I was more uncomfortable with the turnouts than I was with the suit. There were stores in which there'd only be a few people. So after signing an autograph or two, the place would suddenly be empty. Then Fred and the buyer and I would stand around looking at the shelves.

After a lot of work, designing, and talking, the business really took off. A combination of things helped it, not the least of which was the recent extraordinary jump in the popularity of hockey. This also created an increased responsibility for me. The merchandise had to continue to be of a high standard. Sometimes I'd have to goose a manufacturer to maintain quality. I remember some black tape for wrapping sticks that ran. I went to see Fred and I was fuming. My name was on something cheap. Fred made the manufacturer change the color composition, and now the tape doesn't run. There was also a game we put out, and some shipments were defective. I didn't know about it until I started receiving letters from people who had bought these games. You see, when you sell something with your name on it, the public holds you responsible—which it should. So I told the manufacturer to provide them with another game.

I got so wound up in all this that I'd travel around to department stores to see how everything was displayed. If the boxes were arranged sloppily or the equipment wasn't out there, I'd chase after the buyer. Even little things would catch my eye. For example, we used to put green and red bands on our sticks. We changed them when it occurred to me that those weren't the colors of any NHL team.

About this time there was an upsurge of boys playing hockey in the streets. As kids, Tony and I had spent hours at the game. Now on drives through the outskirts of Boston I'd see kids out with a ball and a stick. Also on the way in from the airport in Montreal. They just couldn't get enough hockey.

The most important piece of equipment in street hockey is the plastic blade of your stick. You jammed the shaft of any old broken stick into this and you were in business. That's one reason so many boys are clamoring for our broken sticks after a workout. Usually the blade breaks. But if you have a plastic blade you can stick that on.

There was one essential fault with this blade—if you took a hard shot and hit the sidewalk instead of the puck, the blade might fly off. So Fred and I visited a plastics manufacturer and gave him the idea to work on: what about a screw-on blade? And while he was at it, how about a curve on it as well? The curved stick was the rage. But the only plastic blades available were straight. I remember that as a boy I always wanted to model myself after someone in the NHL. So why not curved plastic blades?

When the first blades were ready, I took them out of the molds myself. I was as excited as a kid. Ideas swirled through my head. Street hockey captured me once again. I could see millions of youngsters playing the game in cities where before it had been only stickball or punchball.

Of course, a second essential was the puck—or something like a puck. A puck is fine for flat surfaces. But most streets are uneven. So a regular puck tends to change direction or tip on its end. Then I remembered what Tony and I had done as kids. We'd take an old tennis ball and punch holes in it until it was dead. This was easier to play with on the street. It still rolled, and would stop dead against the stick. You could also stickhandle and pass it. So Fred and I visited another plastics maker and told him we wanted a ball that would roll—but would stop dead just as soon as it hit the stick. When the first samples arrived I went over to Fred's house and we stickhandled them on the lawn. They worked. And since then we've sold millions.

I knew hockey was big in Scandinavia. I'd even received a few letters from fans there. In 1970, Fred met several Swedes who were interested in putting out a Phil Esposito line for Europe. The next year I spoke with them. To be truthful, the gear wasn't up to our standards, but the Swedes insisted that Europeans would buy it. I agreed, on condition that after a year we'd re-examine the line and redesign it to my specifications. Now we're selling in Sweden, Finland, Holland, Denmark, Germany, England, Switzerland—and even Japan.

Being incorporated doesn't make you shrewd. I still get taken. There was the Puerto Rican trip. When most of these quick-buck guys come around, they don't just have one deal. They've got a dozen, "and this is just the beginning." It was like that with this particular operator. He was going to make me a "consultant" at $15,000 or $20,000 a year. First Puerto Rico. They'd use my name as an attraction to have people sign up for a package deal. It was legitimate. Everyone got their trip all right. But I was supposed to get $2000, as well as a free round trip with my brother, Tony. I didn't ask for the money in advance. It turned out the guy needed 100 people to be able to pay me the $2000. Only 90 showed up. Tony and I didn't know that. When we got back I asked about the money. And a few months later I received $200.

Another group had this brilliant idea: Phil Esposito Safaris. However, I had to put up $1000. "Now let me get this straight," Fred asked them. "You want to use Phil's name in promoting it, you'll use his pictures—and you want him to put up a grand?" We decided against that one.

About then I was buying carpeting for our new house. I met a man with another beautiful scheme. This would be called Phil Esposito's Home Decorating Service. The idea was that this fellow would send salesmen around to homes and give people advice on how to decorate. Then he'd sell them items from our catalogue.

"But what does Phil Esposito have to do with decorating?" Fred asked, together with some other questions. The guy said the business was worth $50,000, but for $10,000 I could own half of it. Well, it was just an idea in the guy's head. We figured it wasn't worth $50,000 in the first place. And second, my $10,000 would be bankrolling the whole thing. Well, that's another one we let slip by.

Most of these fellows are fly-by-night operators. You know, "Meet me on such-and-such a street corner." Actually, that's where we met one guy with whom we were thinking of doing business. Never at an office. Always on some corner. He'd drive by in his Caddy. But after a few meetings, he was driving a Chevvy. We dropped him.

Of course when you get a good deal, you try to take advantage of it. After the big season, Gerry Cheevers, Fred Stanfield, Dennis Hull, and I wanted to go to Las Vegas. Someone told me we could go for free. So I ran to tell all the guys that we'd be going on the arm, including our

wives. I felt like a big shot. Fred wasn't so confident about
the whole thing. He was sure I'd be used in some way.
But I'd promised the fellows a free trip, and I was embarrassed to go back on my word. So Fred got a guarantee
from the promoters of the flight that there'd be no advertising in connection with all this. They agreed. And it was
a heck of a trip. Except when it was over, I got a hotel
bill for $1500.

One promoter wanted to manage me completely. All he
wanted was 5 percent of my salary and 20 percent of outside endorsements. He promised to get me a big raise.
That was a laugh. Did he think after those 126 points I
wouldn't be getting a big raise under the new contract?
What kind of bargain was that? Fred told him, fine, you
get us all the deals you can and we'll give you 20 percent
on a deal-by-deal basis. But we don't want to be tied up.

Actually, we're not interested in everything that comes
along. It's the long buck we want, not the quick one. If
something isn't reputable, or is not a product I believe in,
I won't have anything to do with it. I like "class" endorsements. That's why I listened so attentively when one agent
arrived with a deal from Dodge. They'd use my name to
promote their car, and I'd make a certain number of appearances at conventions and shows. My name wasn't exactly a household word, and we felt the Dodge association
would help. I was to get $1000 a month and two of their
cars for a year. The agent was supposed to pave the way.
But when I went to the advertising office to close the deal,
they asked me what commercials I'd done before. Of

course I had to mention Champion spark plugs—made by a Dodge competitor—but they took me on anyway.

I learned something about being a celebrity that year with Dodge. As I said, the deal was supposed to have me working at auto shows. But I started to get requests from regional managers. One guy wanted me to appear at his son's high school banquet. He figured that if I worked for Dodge I should do that. When I turned him down, he was quite upset.

Being a center of attention has opened my eyes to the way things are in this world. For if you're a celebrity or have a pot of money, people look at you differently. A millionaire and a wage-earner go to the same hotel in Florida, the millionaire gets better treatment. That's just the way it is.

Some of the strangest reactions I received after my record-setting years were from hockey players, past and present. Before the 126 points, or the 76 goals of the 1970–71 season, I was acknowledged as a pretty good player. There wasn't any controversy about me. I was accepted for what I was. But to some individuals, all those points suddenly made me fair game. "I was a big bum; I was a lucky product of expansion; my records were meaningless."

Strange, but criticism always seems to be reserved for those who've had some sort of accomplishment. Until Bobby Hull broke Rocket Richard's record, Richard never rapped the modern hockey player. Then after I did it, he kept talking about "expansion." Well, it's not my fault they went from six teams to 14. Everyone else had the same chance I did. Yet even Larry Hillman, who was playing for the Flyers when I was trying to pass Bobby's record of 58 goals in a season, said, "Esposito's record won't be significant unless he gets 70 goals." So I got 76. Significant. What's that?

But, finally, it's the fans we're playing for. And fans are as different as you'd expect. If one approaches me for an autograph, I try to put myself in his shoes. Although the fan has never met me, he thinks he knows me. Really, all he knows about me is that I'm a hockey player. Nothing else matters. Yet, because he's watched me or heard about me, and knows all my statistics, he feels a certain intimacy that, truthfully, I don't share with him. So when I say no to a fan's request or am surly, he feels he's been slapped in the face or turned down by an old friend. He will remember that one meeting. And if I don't happen to feel good that day, or if he catches me before a game—and I don't sign autographs until after a game—or if he spots me eating in a restaurant with my family and I refuse to sign, then to him I'm a bum. I messed up his one chance at meeting a celebrity.

I now realize that when a fan meets you, he feels he must say something. I don't blame him. Often, a guy comes up and says, "Now, don't let us down—we're counting on you." Does he think I want to lose? Fans feel possessive about a sports figure. He's theirs. At times, I sort of like it. After we won the Stanley Cup in 1970, I was playing in a celebrity golf tournament with Lee Trevino. The crowds got so thick that Trevino said, "A guy could get killed in this mob." I replied, "I play my best in front of a crowd." And I did, too.

Still, there are times I don't like it. Whenever we go out to a restaurant for dinner, I wonder whether we'll get through the meal. Inevitably, someone will come up to me while I'm throwing a forkful of spaghetti into my mouth, and he'll shove a piece of paper in front of me and ask me to sign it.

I'm conscientious about answering fan mail. Over the season I must send out 10,000 color postcards. I figure it costs about $2000. But it's worth it. I enjoy the letters, and I keep them all. Some are fun. Very few are hate letters. A surprising number come from Europe, where there is tremendous interest in the NHL. Here are a few samples:

From 11-year-old Gunilla: "My greatest and only wish is to receive a photo signed by you."

From Peter: "I hope you be well."

From Mary: "My father loves your wrist shot. He doesn't know how you do it. Either do I. My mother is also a great fan of your motions."

From Billy: "My friend said you are a blockhead. I gave him a punch in the nose, he started to cry like a baby."

From Tim: "Excuse the typing my wrightin hand is broken from a accident and I can not wright."

From Gloria: "I am Phil Esposito's hockey stick. If only

you know how it felt when Phil would get out on that ice and wrap his hands around me."

From Speed: "What a nervy bum you are."

And I also get letters which begin: "Your Aunt Ida assured me that you'd help me. . . ."

That's a ticket request. I don't know what the policy is on other teams, but in Boston we get two free tickets for every game and the option to buy two more. On the road, we don't get free tickets. We've got to buy them. Yet, people think we're just looking to give tickets away. Many is the time I've been stuck for tickets after buying them for people who are friends of Aunt Ida, or who come up to me in a hotel lobby and say, "I'm so and so, a friend of a friend. Can you get me a pair for tonight's game?" So I lay out the money, after explaining that the tickets aren't free. The thing is, I'm embarrassed to ask for the money back.

This ticket business is such a pain that I don't even bother with a lot of the free things that come our way: such as suits or shoes or a courtesy car. Because after you get them the fellows want tickets. People just won't believe you can't get tickets. Especially in Boston, which has fewer than 15,000 seats, and most of those belong to season ticket holders.

More than tickets, though, is the public's need to be next to an athlete. I've grown accustomed to people stopping at the house back home. They feel that because they know me I want to have guests around all the time. The same thing happens at marinas wherever I dock my boat.

Someone recognizes me, and there's a crowd. Look, I'm not kidding anyone. There are times when you like adulation. All of us need a certain amount of it. When I was a 17-year-old big shot with the Sarnia Legionairres, I thought I was a hero. We all did, wearing our purple and gold jackets with the crest. That was our badge. And after a game I'd rush out to buy the paper to see my name in it. We all looked for attention. Every boy wants to make a name for himself; he likes the girls coming around.

Of course when it goes, it goes. A former star I know was crying in his beer one night. He was 37 years old and the girls weren't running after him any more. He couldn't understand why the press wasn't coming over and asking his opinions, waitresses didn't flock to him, he wasn't recognized by kids on the street.

Athletes have mixed feelings about their obligations to the public. And I certainly haven't an easy answer. These duties can be as simple as signing an autograph or as difficult as determining which charity dinners to attend. But one thing I won't do: under no circumstance will I sign an autograph in a bar. How would it sound if a kid told his mother that he got my autograph in a bar. Of course I do feel that I have an obligation to be cordial and fair with people, just as anyone does. Yet I've had some bad days, and I suppose the impression I made then is the one people will remember. On the whole, however, I'm a pretty nice fellow.

Yet there's another sort of obligation. And I wonder about this. Am I obliged to attend dinners and charity affairs for free? How do I pick the ones to go to? An athlete has just so many years to make money. Would organizations expect Jerry Lewis or Red Skelton to attend one of their dinners for free? I don't think so. And athletes are show business too.

Since we're presently the most popular team in Boston, we get invitations for every dinner, banquet, and church social. We're invited to weddings, bar mitzvahs, and the confirmations of people we've never even met. I receive more than 100 invitations a year. How do you say no to a charity? It's difficult, but you must draw a line somewhere. So I finally decided to do the charities I feel most strongly about, the ones connected with children.

As for myself, fame also has its bad side. In school I was a big hero. So if I were disciplined, I'd wonder how to react. I knew the other kids were looking to see if I would rebel or take the punishment. That's a lot of pressure for a kid to be under, always to be thinking, "What are people going to say if I do this or do that?" I was constantly aware that there was something special about me, that people knew who I was. On the other hand, I think I can now talk to anyone in the world. I'm used to handling people, to meeting persons from every type of environment. I can't think of a situation that I can't handle. I just step in, put both feet down, and that's it. Call it confidence. I've been there, on the ice with guys hacking and fans screaming and a goaltender trying to stop me, and I've survived.

Yet there were kids back home with all the potential in

the world until fame went to their head. They had no one
to knock it out, like my dad did with me. A lot of these
guys are working in the steel mill and wondering whether
they could have made it. All through their lives they're
going to wonder. They had a little fame and a little money
once, and they became bad actors. They started screwing
around, wasting their talents. Once you get a bad repu-
tation in hockey no one wants to touch you.

I suppose I'd be classified as a medium-bad actor. My
first serious scrape came when I was a junior. You had
to be 21 to drink in Canada, so we went to Niagara Falls,
New York, where you only have to be 18. When I came
back that night, I broke my hotel door. I was sent pack-
ing, after calling the coach a few names. When you're
young, you don't want to be a stick-in-the-mud.

There's a tendency, even after you make it, for teammates to pal around together. We feel more comfortable
because we can be ourselves. We don't have to answer
people who come up and ask, "Hey, are you gonna win
the scoring championship?" That's such a stupid question.
If I knew the answer, I'd quit and become a soothsayer.

Whenever I'm asked a question, I stop and think: what's
the questioner's tone? Is the guy a wiseacre? Is he serious?
Does he want a straight answer?

On a telephone talk show a guy once told me how ter-
ribly I'd played the day before. I got annoyed and asked
him what he did for a living. "I'm a laborer," he said.
"Look," I told him, "I don't tell you how to labor. Don't
tell me how to play hockey." That was the wrong thing

to say. Every laborer in Massachusetts wrote telling me I had some nerve to knock them—which is not what I did. One woman said I had no compassion for the working man. Her letter bothered me. My dad was a laborer, and I'd been one too. I telephoned to apologize. She sent me back a really lovely note.

We don't talk hockey all the time among ourselves. We'll discuss the war or the drug problem. Though we'll discuss hockey, too. But most of us don't want to talk hockey with amateurs. We see the game differently. Still every athlete wonders: is the fan being nice to me for myself or does he want something?

Fame has meant endorsements and a lot of extra money that hockey players never had before. We've never been big-league in the States. So I know exactly what it means. I'm lucky to be hot. It's like that song, "When you're hot, you're hot." You have to take it while you can. When I'm through with hockey no one will ask me for my autograph. I shall disappear like the Roman Empire—and without, perhaps, quite such a lasting impression. So right now I'm nice to everybody. Because, you see, you meet all these people on the way down. And I want them to know me now, while I'm at the top. Maybe it'll help some day.

Earlier I was talking about things I'd learned during my 126-point season. Well, I learned almost as much the following year, when I had 99 points. The fans expected me to score now, so they booed when I didn't. After a while I simply accepted this and did my best. I was bothered, though, when some people said I slumped with a 99-point year. And I emphasize "some." The overwhelming majority of sports fans are truly interested in us, and share our ups and downs. It's a good feeling to hear a fan say after a game, "Nice try," or "Good game," or "We'll get 'em next time."

Believe it or not, we're human. And no matter what guys say after a game, we hear the boos and the insults. But what really upsets me is that so much of the booing is done by kids. Not just booing, but obscenities. There's a group of kids in Philadelphia who spit at the Bruins when we go from the ice to our dressing room. Would you believe such a thing?

I'm convinced that kids get it from their parents. Somewhere along the way the father or mother took their son to a hockey game and the boy heard the parent cursing or threatening us. Sometimes it's hard not to rush right into the stands after the guy.

Of course every fan has the right to boo. If he can cheer us for his $6, then he should be able to let us know when he's not happy. A bad play in basketball may receive some booing, or in football or baseball. Still it won't continue for long. But in hockey the fans seem more caught up in the action. Maybe because we're so close to the people, or the game's so fast and violent. And if the best team in the world has a bad game, the fans let you know it. Then, just as suddenly, they rush to your side if the game turns around. On the ice you catch this change. The crowd is very much a part of the game. It can goose you into high gear, or it can make you feel miserable.

Wherever you are, you hear the fans, though usually you don't acknowledge them. But sometimes you turn around. That's a fatal mistake. You give a guy in the stands a sign, and he's beaten you—even though the sign you gave him doesn't mean "hello." The fans who scream don't realize that it doesn't bother us. Often, in fact, it just psyches us up more.

Still I hope they don't now expect me to get 76 goals and 152 points every season, like 1971. Though naturally I shall try.

4

The Violence

Sometimes I think I'm not mean enough. Perhaps I should be meaner. For when you set a scoring record you become the target for every hatchet man in the league. We have "shadows," guys whose job it is to follow us around the ice whenever we're on. The shadow may not even be a regular, the coach just suits him up to guard a certain player. A shadow isn't necessarily a hatchet man. He can cling to you and still be clean. But his job is to stop you from scoring; and the referees always seem to let the clutchers and grabbers get away with it when they're tying up a name player.

Watching Bobby Hull when I was with Chicago, I'd say to myself, "Holy God, how does he stand it?" Can you imagine what would happen if Bobby did the same things to his opponents? And the refs just let it go. One referee said to me, "When you become a superstar you've got to expect that to happen."

The worst defensemen hold you in front of the net. They can't body you out of the way, and they can't stop you from getting the puck. You want to scream when they're clutching at you and you've got a hell of a chance at a goal and you're fouled and the ref says nothing. Yet, I suppose if I were playing against me I'd try it, too.

The holders are frustrating, but they're not the most dangerous. Still you've got to remember that what happens in hockey happens quickly: bodies are moving, each player carries a stick and is wearing skates with edges sharp as razors, while all the time a hard rubber puck is flying around. The danger and the violence are always there. You know what can happen: you can be tripped into the boards and bust your neck. They can butt-end you and rupture your spleen. Why guys even come up from behind and crack you across the back with their stick. From the stands it doesn't look so bad. But you've got no protection there. And believe me, you're whistling Dixie.

Those who swing their sticks are the absolute worst. No one respects them. It's ugly. If you've ever seen a stick-fight you know what I mean. Like the one between Teddy Green and Wayne Maki. We kid Greenie now about the plate in his head. But if we didn't, the strain would tell.

Some goalies use their sticks, too. When you're skating after the puck at full speed and a goalie raps you across the ankle, you're down. Ken Hodge broke an ankle against Minnesota when Cesare Maniago, the North Stars' goalie, took a swipe at him and cracked a bone in Ken's foot.

There are also those dodos who spear you in front of the net. They figure the ref can't see it because there's usually such a commotion going on near the goalie. Of course, there are accidents. But when a guy stabs you with his stick, and he's carrying it like a pitchfork—well, you know it's no accident. The front of the net is where the worst action takes place. It's like the pit in football. And it's a matter of survival out there. You're on your own. Don't expect help from the referee—he can't see what's happening. Besides cracking you across the back, some guys get you behind the knee and you're down. It doesn't take much. Remember, we're all pretty strong and what looks like a love tap from the stands is making you moan on the ice.

There are some notorious clutchers and grabbers—including Dale Rolfe, Larry Hillman, Ed Van Impe, and Terry Harper. These guys have one thing in common: they're pretty tall and they're all arms.

Stick-fighters are in a different class. Everyone knows who'll drop his stick and who won't. Sometimes on the bench you'll hear: "Be careful of that guy. He won't drop his stick."

Elbows are part of the game. Gordie Howe was a great one for that. You'd be backchecking him and all of a sudden you've got an elbow in the face. No one saw it because he could dig it in so quickly. But when you're a scorer you want to establish right away that you're not going to let the other guy get away with anything. A little elbow never hurt.

Gordie really broke me in. There was a face-off, I went for the puck, and came out of it with five stitches. There was a scuffle, and we went off to the penalty box together. "And you used to be my idol," I told him.

I think the last time I really lost my temper was in a game against Philadelphia. It started simply enough. I had a fight with Larry Hale and we threw a few punches. As we broke up, Referee Bob Sloan skated toward us. Just then Hale said something to me and I replied, "Bug off." Sloan thought I had spoken to him. He handed me a 10-minute misconduct penalty and I went berserk. I punched him twice.

After meeting with Campbell and giving my side of the story, I received a two-game suspension. I hadn't said anything nasty to Sloan, and was angry simply because I'd gotten a penalty I didn't deserve. When you're brought before Campbell on charges such as striking an official, however, films are reviewed and testimony is taken from the referee and two linesmen. One of the linesmen told Campbell he'd heard me swear at Sloan, which I never did. But his testimony was thrown out when the films showed he was at the other end of the ice.

When hockey players get into a fight, only a few of them are truly afraid. Because the worst that can happen is that you'll lose. Injuries are rare. Maybe a tooth or two; but you don't really think about it. It's not so much that we're impervious to pain, it's just that if the occasion arises—well, you've got to protect yourself. Most of the punching and wrestling you see from the stands has just one effect: it tires the guy who's throwing the punches. Since you can't set to throw a punch on the ice as easily as you can in a boxing ring, you can't land the punch. So the punches miss or hit the guy's shoulder where he's protected. And all the while you're sparring and looking for an opening, you're sliding around on the ice. I think the worst I've ever received in such a fight was a black eye.

One of hockey's clichés is that you can't score from the penalty box. That's true. I'm not paid to sit and watch the action. I'm paid to score goals. Stan Mikita realized this after spending 154 minutes in the penalty box one season. That's practically three whole games. Two years later he lowered the total to 12 minutes and won both the scoring championship and the Lady Byng Trophy for clean play. It's hard not to fight back. You want to retaliate, because you can't let anyone take liberties with you. But there's a right time and a wrong time. Remember: when you're in the box you're of no use to anybody. And your team must play shorthanded.

There is, however, another side to fighting: your pride. It hurts when you lose a fight and your own teammates rib you. And don't think we don't. If a guy loses a fight and he's not too badly hurt, he knows he's going to hear about it. Maybe it's because we tend to turn something bad into something humorous. Like Ted Green's injury. I think a guy loosens up when he comes back to the bench with a black eye and we tell him, "Tape an aspirin on it— you'll survive." If he can laugh about losing the fight, maybe he won't stew over it. A lot of times in practice someone will get hit with the puck or maybe crash into the boards and get up slowly. You're sure to hear someone say, "Come on, now—the TV's not on you."

When Rick Smith played for us he had a fight with Dan Maloney, and Maloney really whacked him with a great punch. I had to admire it. Later, we laughed about it in the dressing room and Rick joined us. "That's one punch I'll never forget," he said.

A team is like a family. You have to get along and share each other's good times and troubles. One bad apple can screw up a team. I've always tried to be friendly with everyone on the club. I used to feel pretty awful when I was breaking in and some of the regulars wouldn't speak to me.

On the road we tend to stay together. At home we're almost inseparable. This of course is during the season. After practices we'll go for a beer and a sandwich. After games we get together with our wives for dinner out. The Bruins have always been an especially close club. We've never had cliques. I saw that on Chicago and I didn't like it. You know: three guys from the same line always palling around together; or a few players who were together in juniors. I think being close off the ice helps a team during games. You'll pull for a fellow to score, and get really high when a teammate reaches the 20-goal mark or gets a hat trick. It's a good feeling.

I even talk to the opposition. A lot of guys—and coaches —think it's wrong. But that's old-fashioned. If two businessmen can talk together and then hustle each other's business, why can't two athletes do the same? I'm close to my brother. Still that doesn't stop me from trying to get as many goals as I can against him. He's the enemy. I feel the same way about players who've been traded away. I'll have a beer with any of them and enjoy it. But we'll still go after each other when there's a game on. Fans can't seem to understand this: that what we're doing on the ice is simply a job we try to do as best we can. I'm not going to hate a guy just because he gives me a body check.

Whenever you find a great team in sports, everyone's pulling together. And this is one reason for our success. Yet, I think we've been drifting away from each other. We don't go out for beers together as much as we used to. We've all got some measure of fame now and suddenly we find we're more in demand. This tends to keep us apart. Success, I suppose, leads to this. Still I hope we'll be able to recapture what we once had.

It's easier to feel a part of things these days. Expansion has seen to that. Now there's nothing unusual about a rookie making the team. But when I broke in with the Hawks, I don't think there were more than three rookies even trying for spots on the club. I got the cold shoulder. In those days, there weren't many positions open in the NHL—there were six teams and about 100 players. Every guy guarded his own spot. A rookie was a potential threat. If he took your job away, there weren't many places to go. Maybe that's why rookies were ignored. The veterans felt you had to prove yourself before they accepted you.

Some guys didn't want to make friends in training camp. They figured that half the guys they met wouldn't be around by the time the regular season began. Only three Hawks spoke to me when I was trying to make the club—Bobby Hull, Reggie Fleming, Chico Maki. Stan Mikita and I seldom talked. Bill Hay never said much to me either. Come to think of it, Mikita and Hay were centers, like me. I wonder if that was it. But neither did Pierre Pilote go overboard to be nice to me—and he was the club's captain. He was also a defenseman.

Because expansion has created more than 300 NHL jobs, we aren't so uptight. Any decent player can wind up somewhere. Also with the World Hockey Association coming along in 1972 and lots of us being approached to jump leagues, this has made it even easier.

Unless a rookie is real cocky, I'll invite him along for a beer with the guys. I remember what it was like when I broke in, and I'm glad to make life easier for a youngster.

Although I consider the guys on my team like family, this doesn't mean I consider the opposition my enemy. But Keith Magnuson of the Hawks, I understand, psyches himself up before a game by concentrating on hating the other team. He goes into a real frenzy. My brother Tony, the Hawks' goalie, won't talk to me on the day we're playing each other. Yet, we'll have dinner together the night before.

From stories I've heard, John Ferguson of the Canadiens was just like Magnuson. In fact, Fergy wouldn't even talk to guys on other teams when the season was over. Until he retired, he'd never attend a banquet if there was somebody from another team on the dais with him. But he was pretty clever. Because when he was playing, he would never just explode. Instead, he'd carefully calculate when would be a good time to start a fight, or draw a rough penalty. Once when the Canadiens were playing the Black Hawks, Claude Ruel, the Montreal coach, told Fergy to "start something." So Fergy punched Bobby Hull.

Yet, for all I know, John Ferguson was a hell of a guy. Fans find it difficult to believe that a player can be violent on the ice, real nasty, acting like a punk—and not be just exactly that. I admit I'm guilty. I make judgments about a person strictly from his behavior on the ice. How many people will believe me when I tell them that Teddy Green is one of the nicest guys you'd ever hope to meet? Bruin fans accept it because they're rooting for him. But a fan from another city, or a player from another team? Never. They've got a picture of what Greenie must be like—based strictly on the fact that he's a pretty tough customer in a hockey game.

Can we separate our private lives from the violence on the ice? I think I do it pretty well, though Linda helps a lot. We agreed during our first year of marriage that hockey was going to be my job, but that it wouldn't control our home life. So she never brings up anything at home that's happened to me in a game. Linda is happier this way; she'd rather keep her thoughts to herself. Still I know she's aware how I feel after a bad game, since she tells the girls to be quiet. And on the day of a game she takes the phone off the hook.

We used to let our older daughter, Laurie, watch the first period on television. But the next day she'd often ask me if I'd scored a goal, and we decided to cut out her game-watching completely. At age 7 Laurie shouldn't be concerned whether her father scores or not. We know she's aware there's something special about what I do, and that people talk about it. Because once she came home from school crying that a kid in her class had called me a bum. Linda has tried to explain that I have a special sort of job and that people say good things and bad things about me. But in spite of the care we take, Laurie will still occasionally say, "That man really hit you last night." And I'll know she's seen a bit of the game somehow.

As much as possible, we try to lead a normal life. We're settled in a home. Some players never live permanently where they play, especially in American cities. They rent houses, and never really feel a part of the community. But we bought a house as soon as I was traded to Boston.

Again, some players put their families through a strange routine: they have their kids start school in Canada in September, during the training-camp season, only to switch to schools in the States. Then when the season is over in April or May (depending on whether you make the playoffs), they take the kids back home to finish school in Canada. On some clubs, three-quarters of the guys must do it this way. They have lesson plans sent from one school to the other, and the parents know at what stage the Canadian kids are, and whether their own children at school in the States are keeping pace. But Laurie has always started and finished school in Lynnfield, Massachusetts, and Carrie, who's three years younger, will too.

I know this sounds like any normal family—which is a big thing for me. I hope Linda and the kids will always be involved in what I do, but I don't want it to become a burden to them. I want them to know I'm still a father and a husband. If they see me get angry on the ice, or if they see others become violent, I want them to understand that that's a part of me I try to leave behind. Linda isn't comfortable in the public eye. But she's become philosophical about it. She'd like to finish a meal in a restaurant or walk quietly with a shopping cart, yet she knows all this other will help the kids: that the education they'll receive just meeting so many different people will benefit them as they grow older.

She insists on going back to Canada for the summer, though, to our cottage on the Soo peninsula. Here, where it's quiet, we return to our real home after the winter. And everything is peaceful.

5

On the Road

People may think it's a bed of roses on the road. But it's a boring, boring time. For me, Los Angeles and Oakland are the best. Not because there's the Sunset Strip in L.A. or San Francisco across the Bay—but because nobody knows you. You can take in a little sightseeing. Or you can do something as simple as having breakfast quietly. Now this may not sound like such a big deal. But when you're in a city to play a game that night, breakfast and lunch become the major social events of your day. You like to spend the time with the guys. In Montreal, for instance, you can't believe the crowd that follows us around absolutely everywhere. In Minnesota or L.A. I may be sitting in a coffee shop and a fan walks up to me and says, "I came all the way from Boston to see you." And then he wants an autograph or some tickets. Well, if he's come all that distance you've got to be civil to him. But sometimes I prefer room service.

The road is more than just a fact of life for hockey players today—it's a whole way of life. When I came up there were six teams. We were the most western club; yet travel was incredibly simple. Our longest trip was from Chicago to Boston, about 850 miles. The absolute worst we'd have would be an overnight train ride. Most of the time, we'd arrive in a city the morning of a game. There were only five other clubs, and now it seems like a lark, with 70 games. Some teams still traveled a lot by train in the early sixties—especially the Canadiens. In fact they always traveled by train before expansion. After expansion in 1967, they switched to planes; but after one near-disaster the club went back to trains as much as possible. Their goalie, Gump Worsley, never could stand flying. Here was a goalie in the NHL, one of the most hazardous jobs in sport, and he would practically cry before getting on a plane. Gump was a guy who'd never wear a goalie's mask, yet he had to be lubricated before boarding. When he quit the Canadiens, he said he couldn't take the flying. But then a psychiatrist helped him out.

Train travel saved the teams money. Some clubs would use the train as their hotel. Say you played a game in Toronto on Wednesday and had a game in Detroit the next night. The train would rest on a siding. After the game the guys would climb aboard, spend the night there, and then get off in Detroit the next morning.

Now we go everywhere by plane. We have to. Vancouver, Minnesota, St. Louis, Atlanta, Buffalo—you name it, we play there. We fly 70,000 miles a year. A reporter told me that he's exhausted after the season—and he hasn't even suited up for a game. Doctors say it takes two solid days before you get really accustomed to the time change when you travel across the country by jet. How'd you like to arrive in Oakland at 5 P.M. one day and then play a hockey game the next night? And then follow that a day later with a game at L.A. and then one at Vancouver?

But of all the guys on our team, Derek Sanderson was the only one who complained about the flying. At least, he was the only one to admit he didn't like it. So Derek might take a sleeping pill before a flight. But I know lots of fellows who are really afraid to go up, and that adds to the mental strain. You see, in hockey it's not the physical aspects of travel and being on the road that get you—it's the mental part. And when you're doing 70,000 miles of travel a year and you don't like it up in the air, well, that's pretty exhausting.

Take 300 people from any business and the chances are there'd be a few who simply refuse to fly. But in hockey we all fly. Why? Because where else are we going to earn this sort of money. You've only got until you're 36 or 37 to make it. Also, hockey is in our blood. The incentive to play is so great that it outweighs any fear one might have of flying. When I was a kid I played when it was 10° below because it was important to me to play. And that desire to keep playing stays right with you.

Once you've arrived in a city there's not much to do. It's either a movie, or a drink, or a meal, or sleeping. We're not in a town long enough really to enjoy it. And we've got a game to play.

The routine works something like this: say it's Tuesday in Boston and we've got a game in Detroit the next night. We catch a plane about 5 or 6 P.M. We get to our hotel in Detroit by 9 o'clock. The night's shot. In the morning, you sleep pretty late, say till 10. Then there's breakfast. Most teams have a meeting at the rink at noon. We don't. All this time you feel like a traveler, an outsider. You've got your suit pack back in your room and you're really not part of the scene.

Next comes lunch. Only we call it "the steak." That's because no matter where you are, no matter how hungry you are (or aren't) you eat a steak for lunch. That's the way it's always been. I've never known anyone to eat fish for lunch, even though there may be as much protein in it. After the steak comes the nap. Most of us sleep for a few hours before a game. At first you don't think you'll ever get used to it, just falling asleep in the early afternoon. But it's such a part of our routine that it becomes easy. I like to nap between 3 and 4, but no longer than an hour. I feel logy if I sleep too long. So I put my head on the pillow and I'm out.

After the nap, we get our stuff together and meet in the lobby. Our luggage is then stowed on the team bus (the trainer has already taken our equipment to the rink) and we're off.

For some reason, it always seems the plane we have to catch leaves 90 minutes after the game. That gives us just time to unwind for a few moments before the press comes in, talk to them, shower, and leave in the team bus for the airport. Very rarely do we ever stay over in a town.

If we've got a game the following day, by league rules we must be on our way the night before. The one exception is when we're going from Boston to New York. Then we generally leave Boston that morning. But otherwise, we clear out of a city quick. Either we head for the next place we're playing or return home, if we've got a few days open or if our next game is back in Boston.

On the flight out of town, we have a steak. Some fellows can sleep, but most of the guys need time to wind down, especially the goalies. If we've got a game the following night it's rough. Say we play in St. Louis or Minnesota or Chicago one night, then play back east the next. You're on the plane by 11 or 11:30, but you don't arrive at your destination until 2 in the morning, local time. When you reach your hotel room it's 3 A.M. Then you still think about the game. Of course you're tired the next night, although you play because that's what you're supposed to do.

But what about a televised afternoon game? You got to bed at 3 A.M., you're up at 10, and you must be out on the ice at 2 in the afternoon.

The schedule takes a toll. When the oldtimers rap today's players they don't know what they're talking about. Until the end of World War II it was a 50-game schedule. Now it's 78 games, all over North America. And we may play four or five nights a week.

By January I'm pretty bored with things. It's midseason and hockey is coming out of my ears. When I get to this stage, I'd sooner play every day than practice once. The practice is almost pointless. You're doing the same things time after time and you have to search for incentive. But then the All-Star game comes along and suddenly I've got my second wind. Once again, the pennant race is on.

I don't know how goalies stand it. My brother Tony played more than 60 games one year and the pressure just about drove him nuts. That's why there's the two-goalie system today. No goaltender wants to play every game. And with the slap shot and the curved stick, the puck does tricks. It curves or rises or dips. So goalies must wear masks these days simply to survive.

The real danger on the road to all of us, however, is the potential riot situations in such rinks as Philadelphia, Detroit, and Chicago. Here there's precious little security after a game while the fans mill around, pushing and shoving, hoping to get autographs. It's really frightening. You're perfectly willing to sign autographs, but in Chicago and Detroit you can't. Things are completely out of hand.

Each city is somewhat different, although my game remains pretty much the same. Still, there are noticeable dissimilarities in the rinks and the fans.

New York. It's a toss-up between New York and Philadelphia for obscenities. Even when I'm crossing Seventh Avenue to the Garden I hear them. I'm not interested in seeing the city. The place is too big; it gobbles you up. Oh sure, when I first broke in with Chicago I did the sightseeing bit—the Statue of Liberty, the Empire State Building. But now we're not in New York long enough. We take the 10 A.M. shuttle and we're in our hotel by noon. I'll go to a movie if I can find company; I don't like going by myself. There are very few good restaurants near the Garden. And the waiters and waitresses aren't exactly friendly. Another thing—the ice is pretty bad. And when you've got bad ice it's not only harder to skate but the puck bounces crazily as well. With so many ruts and everyone skating all out, someone's going to get seriously hurt in that town.

Philadelphia. The City of Brotherly Love has great room service; and I usually play well at the Spectrum. But their security is the worst. You'd think that after all the trouble they've had—with the big fight during the 1972 season between St. Louis and the fans—something would be done. However, except for the NHL announcing that it would look into security measures at the various rinks, little has happened. Otherwise, Philadelphia is a good place for me to catch up on such books as *The Godfather* or *The Adventurers.* There's certainly nothing else to do.

Pittsburgh. Have you ever been to Pittsburgh? Jack Riley, the Penguins' executive director, describes it as "a shot and a glass of beer." No disagreement here.

Minnesota. These fans really know their hockey. And one of the North Stars, Lou Nanne, is a particular friend of mine. Lou went to school in the state and now makes his home out there where he's quite a hero. I often eat dinner at his home the night before a game. And Lou spends time with us, too. Lou also hails from the Soo; and we've always maintained our early friendship. Minnesota fans are very much like the Canadians. They tend to be quiet. I remember their first year in the league when Wren Blair, the general manager, tried to hype things up. "The fans don't cheer enough," he said. "And they will applaud a good play no matter who makes it." Blair was trying to tell them not to be neutral, that they had to be involved. The Metropolitan Sports Center is a handsome arena with two distinct types of fans: the Establishment crowd in their blazers from the wealthy suburbs, like Edina; and the Expansion crowd who have spent the day snowmobiling and arrive wearing heavy sweaters under bulky parkas. Walter Bush, the team's president, calls them the thousand-dollar millionaires. I received a silver stick in Minnesota for winning the scoring championship. The crowd gave me a tremendous ovation. So perhaps I'm partial.

St. Louis. The Blues have tremendous fans. I used to play there, and some of them remember me. The club also has a policy of periodically cleaning out the most abusive gallery baiters. I like that. Most rinks make no effort to discourage these people. And lastly, whether the team is losing or not, the Blues get a standing ovation before every period. Now that really would be nice.

Montreal. No relaxing there. It's so close to Boston that many fans come up from home and you're always recognized. If you pop into a bar for a beer, a dozen spies call the coach. Actually, the day before a game we're allowed a drink or two; as long as we're in before curfew—11 or 11:30—it's okay. If we miss curfew, there's a $500 fine. Fortunately, Eddie Johnston has found a quiet little place where it's dark and we go unrecognized. Otherwise, I played my first game with Chicago at the Forum. And the Canadiens have a habit of winning there.

Toronto. You'd think such an old rink as Maple Leaf

Gardens would have great ice. But it's as bad as New York's. Snow all over the place. One good thing, the fans don't get hysterical. They sit on their hands. That doesn't bother us. We're the visitors. But the Toronto management says it's like playing 78 road games a year. Perhaps it's just because so many players on the other teams come from the Toronto area; and that with so many of their friends and relatives at the games, the audience tends to be somewhat impartial and the opposition is especially up. But it's pretty much all the same to me.

Vancouver. The rink needs a few more light bulbs. My God, we practically have to feel our way around the place. And everyone wears a raincoat because it rains all the time. Our favorite spots are Oil Can Harry's and the Cave.

Oakland. The Golden Seals have some rabid fans. Given a winning club, they'll turn voracious. Yet I received a standing ovation there when I tied Bobby Hull's record of 58 goals. Under Garry Young, the general manager, the Seals cleaned house and now have the youngest team in hockey. Of course it's not much fun to play before 3000 or 4000 fans. But things are bound to get better.

Los Angeles. I like warm weather, so I like this city as much as any place we play. Of course a lot of teams make the mistake of lounging around the beach or at pools before a game. But we don't do that. Can you imagine putting on all our equipment over a sunburn? I go into my room and turn on the air conditioner. Then the TV. There's great television in Los Angeles. And when we walk around nobody knows us. Of course I've got a special feel-

That was back in January
'71 against the Kings, and
I'd just scored my fifth
hat trick of the season.

Here I'm slipping one past Toronto's Bernie Parent.

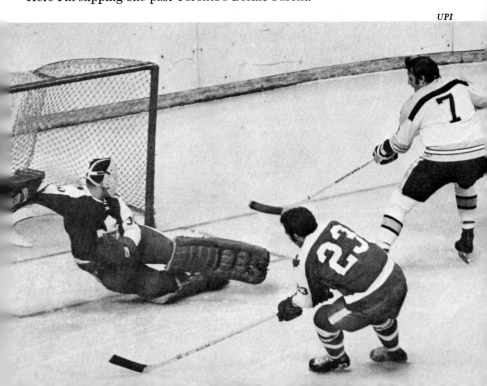

'71 again, and in pretty distinguished company: Bobby Hull and Gordie Howe, with Park and Orr down the table.

I do seem to be carrying on a bit here, but this was goal number 59 in '71. A pretty big one for me.

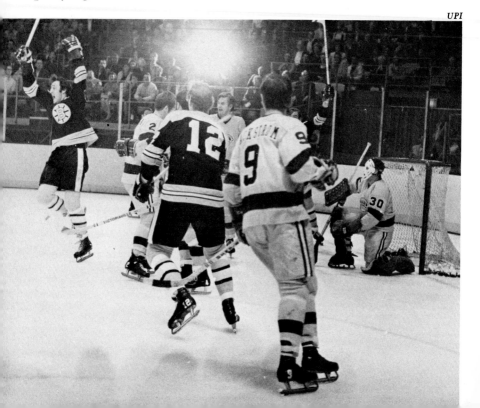

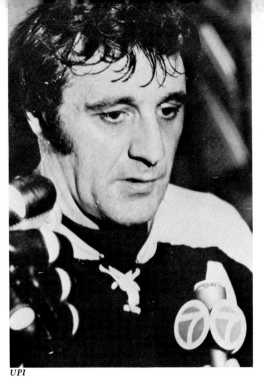

Of course the press wanted
to know all about it.

Gump Worsley and the
North Stars.

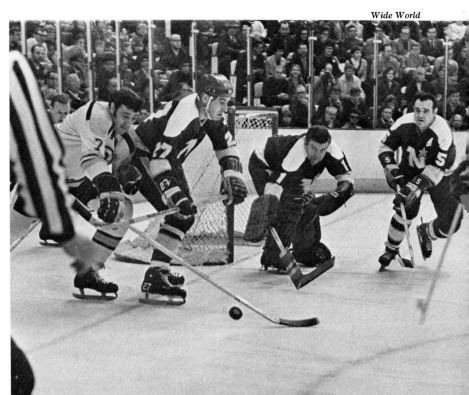

Al Ruelle

Mom, Dad, Tony, and me.

That's Dale Rolfe trying to block the shot. But my eyes say he missed.

Al Ruelle

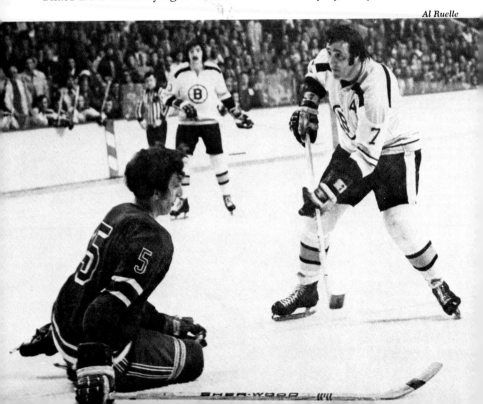

Mark Ofstein

Hockey school.

With Bobby.

Damned if Dryden didn't keep it out. Bobby and I were sure pressing him though.

A winning night, I'd guess.

Oh, those were my early street
hockey pucks.

Al Ruelle

The Blues are really giving me the
business. Right in my favorite spot,
too.

UPI

Both photos by Al Ruelle

Every now and then I make a little pitch for my equipment.

Well, I guess you can guess who we are.

A couple of All-Stars.

This one looks by Minnesota's Cesare Maniago.

Which about says it.

Al Ruelle

Ragging it.

UPI

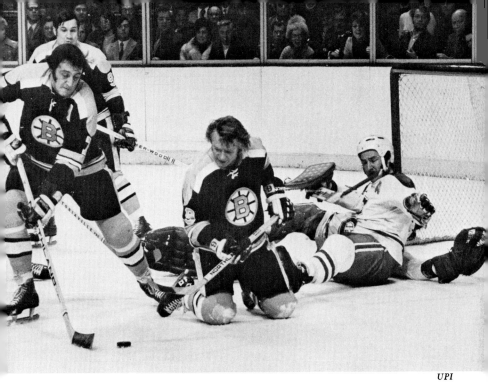

Can't remember whether Pie and I got this one past Dryden or not. But he looks pretty well out of it.

I really like spending time with the kids.

At a practice session just before we took on Toronto in the
'72 playoffs. The moustache is Derek.

Parent stopped this one, and Toronto nipped us 4-3 in overtime.

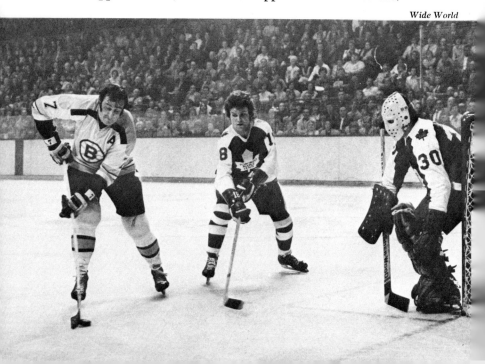

That was against the Blues in the semifinals.

Although we beat New York in the finals, they did manage to tie me up on occasion. 18 is Tkaczuk, my shadow.

Gerry is one hell of a goalie,
and well worth listening to.

Al Ruelle

New York and the finals, again, with good old Walter still tailing me. Oh,
you know who the others are.

UPI

The cup was greeted with affection after we took the Rangers. Ken Hodge waits his turn.

ABC Fabrikerna Kungälv

Fred Sharf and I check headgear production in Sweden.

I stuffed this one by Tretiak in Toronto, as we beat Russia 4-1 to even our series.

I'll never forget that moment in Moscow.

ing for the Forum, since that's where I scored my 59th goal to break Hull's record. A lot of older fellows such as Harry Howell, Ralph Backstrom, Bob Pulford, and Denis DeJordy wind up in L.A.; and they love it. Howell even turned down a $50,000-a-year contract to coach the New York Raiders of the WHA in order to stay out there. No first-year coach ever received that kind of an offer before. Still it's strange seeing hockey fans in white pants and sun tans.

Chicago. These fans can be mean. If they don't take to you, you're in deep trouble. Like Dennis Hull. But if you catch their fancy, as Lou Angotti did, then you can't do anything wrong. I get a strange satisfaction when I'm booed in Chicago. It feels good. Players like to do well against a team that's traded them, and when they boo me it must mean they think I'm hurting their club enough to warrant their boos. The crowd is big and loud. And it's probably as representative of the city as any in the NHL. It's the only arena I know that sells standing-room by location.

Detroit. The Olympia is impossible. As I said, there's going to be a riot there some day if they don't tighten up the security precautions.

Buffalo. The first year the Sabres were in the league, 1970–71, their arena was a dinky little place. But now they've increased the seating capacity and it's a very loud crowd. Buffalo is one of the few arenas where you see black fans. In general the crowd looks as if it had just finished work at the shop. Not many suits. About 60 percent of the fans come from the other side of the border. That's why you'll hear a lot of cheering for players like Derek, who comes from St. Catherines, practically a Buffalo suburb. Sinatra's is our favorite hangout. But over-all, Buffalo isn't one of the most exciting places.

6

Facing Reality

I was 8 years old when the guidance counselor came to my school and asked us what we wanted to be. I said I wanted to be a hockey player, and she said, "That's fine—but what do you want to do?"

At 4 I got my first skates. Double-runners. It was like slippery shoes. Out back, Dad built a rink for Tony and me. There were no sideboards; we'd just pile the snow around the edges. So when spring came and the snow melted, we found dozens of pucks that we'd lost during the winter.

As I got older hockey became more and more the focus of my life. I'd come home from school at 3 and skate till 5:30. Maybe that's why my marks were so bad. I'd think about the game all the time. When I came in for supper, I wouldn't even take off my skates. Then I'd go out and play again until it was so dark we couldn't see. You develop quick reflexes playing in the dead of night. And we'd play our games everyplace—in parking lots, basements, the sidewalks, the yard. Our favorite game was called "Pump, pump, pullaway." One guy would stand in the middle of the ice. He was "it." Then all the other guys had to skate from one end of the rink to the other without being tagged by the fellow in the middle. I'd make it most of the time. Maybe that's where I developed my dekes and fakes—one guy trying to touch me, and I trying to get around him.

This may also explain the way I hold the puck. I used to "rag" it a lot, cradling the puck on my stick and daring the other kids to take it away. I'd play imaginary games in which a team was bearing down on me and trying to take the puck. I'd test my friends on face-offs and stick-handling, and finally got to the point where I almost never lost the puck. I'm pretty good at cradling the puck; though I'm at my best on face-offs or stickhandling when we have the man advantage. I just know I'm not going to get beat on the draw or lose the puck while I'm skating the power play.

When the snow was on the ground we were at our happiest. But in spring we simply traded our skates for shoes, and played street hockey. I'd go through four pairs of shoes over the summer. Any day it went below 80°, we'd be out there on the street, knocking the ball around.

Hockey was everything to us. We had no television. Basketball and baseball and football we simply read about. But when hockey was on the radio—and we could pick up the Toronto and Detroit games—we'd crowd around and listen to the Leafs' Foster Hewitt or the Wings' Budd

Lynch and our day was made. Kids today may find it hard to realize how excited we got just listening to the radio. What with TV and all. But there was something even more magical in not actually being able to see our heroes. All week long I'd play hockey. And then on Saturday night I'd listen to a real game and I could see them all clearly in my mind.

When I was 7 or 8 my uniforms were all Red Wing red with a big Number 9 (Gordie Howe's number) on the back. When one wore out, I'd get another just like it. By the time I hit my teens, Jean Beliveau was hockey's big center, so I decided that was going to be my position. Then nothing would do but that I should wear Beliveau's Number 4. Still, there will always be a special place for Gordie. He was my first idol. After the 1968–69 season I received my first All-Star selection at center. The man I beat out for the position was Jean Beliveau. And my feelings were somewhat mixed.

You hear us complain about the All-Star game money, or how much we don't make in the playoffs. Fans hate this. And it's as distasteful to me as it is to them. But, damnit, I'm a professional with only about ten years to sock it away and I have to look at the game differently.

We receive our salaries in much the same way as I did when I drove a truck. I get a check every two weeks. And though our contracts usually run for a year, the money is paid from the start to the end of the regular season. Every two weeks, we receive a check. Say a player receives

$50,000 a year and the income isn't deferred or spread out. About October 15 he'll get his first check. And since there are about 12 paydays a season, he'll gross about $4,000 each time.

Once a player reaches that salary, he should know how to handle it. But what about the fellow making $20,000 a year. He gets those 10 or 12 paychecks, and each one is a whopper. Of course there are withholding taxes, but that's still a sizable chunk of money. So the guy figures he can blow a thousand and in two weeks he'll be getting just as much again. But what many players forget is that the money stops coming in during April, May, June, July, August, and September. Six months. Yet, some fellows spend the money as if the checks would be coming in all the time. So they're living as though they made twice as much money as they really do. Six months without a check is a long time. That's why I used to drive a truck. Of course if you make the playoffs, there'll be a June check. But you've got to have some confidence to bet on that in October.

Every player receives exactly the same salary for the exhibitions. Would you believe $60 a game? That's right. We get $600 for the 10-game exhibition slate. I don't see the owners charging the fans any less for these games. At every NHL rink the prices are just the same as they are for regular season. Some rinks, in fact, even make their subscribers buy tickets to these practice sessions.

During training camp we also get meal money, $12 a day. This is given to us in cash by the coach. That's not too bad in London, Ontario, where you can get a steak for $5 or $6. But during the regular season, it's tough to eat on the $17 we then receive. Anyone who's ever lived out of a suitcase can tell you that.

Still, there's no comparison with the way it used to be. I suppose the recently formed Players Association is largely responsible for that. The association has helped to raise the minimum salary from $7500 to $12,000, and also to increase the Stanley Cup money. Over-all, it's been a tremendous boon. The counseling available to players, the endorsements—everything has turned out well. The players today are united, and the association is strong.

The All-Star game pay is still a disgrace. Besides the money which is small, the game comes in the middle of the season when the guys are tired. They're concerned about injuries—that's when they happen. And there's half a season to play—the tough half—followed by the playoffs. Why not stage the game after the season, like they do in pro football?

A funny thing about All-Star games. Even though we're supposed to be a bunch of egocentric stars, a lot of passing goes on, as if no one wants to be labelled a hog. Take me. I'm a center. And I get off more shots than anyone else. But I've played with Frank Mahovlich, Gordie Howe, Bobby Hull, Yvan Cournoyer in these All-Star games. Now you know I'm not going to pig the puck with such great shooters around.

Besides All-Star game money, there's also All-Star team money, which is something very different. At the end of each season, the Professional Hockey Writers Association votes several awards, and they're worth a certain amount. But it's the honor which really counts. There's the Hart Trophy, for the most valuable player, and there's also the All-Star team balloting. The Art Ross Trophy goes automatically to the scoring champion.

You hear lots of stories about what the Stanley Cup means to players—that it's a new season, that you can throw out the regular season, that it's a tougher grind mentally and physically. Well, it's all true.

When you play in the final round, it's a completely new experience. You think you know what nervous is. But you don't. The smallest mistake can wipe out the whole year. Before, if we lose four games in a seven-game stretch we can come back and reel off 20 games without a defeat. Not in the Stanley Cup. Four in seven and you're out.

If you lack confidence you're in trouble. Early on with the Hawks I took a rap as a bad playoff performer. And I'll say this, Billy Reay didn't help me a bit. I can win about 80 percent of my face-offs, even more when we're on a power play. But every time we had a clutch face-off, Billy would put someone else out there.

Maybe that's why my playoff record looks so awful at the beginning; this kid's first series with the Hawks shows 4 games played, no goals, and no assists. It also shows no penalty minutes. I sat on the sidelines. Yet, the figures show 0 for 4.

In 1965, we played 13 games and I got 3 goals and 3 assists. Not bad, but not particularly good either. However, in 1966, I was bad—1 goal in 6 games. But everyone on the Hawks was pretty bad that year. Or maybe it was Roger Crozier, Detroit's goalie, who went on to win the Conn Smythe Trophy for his outstanding playoff performance. Against the Maple Leafs in 1967, who had Terry Sawchuk and Johnny Bower, I got nothing in six games. Then I was traded. So in 29 playoff games with the Hawks my record shows 4 goals and 4 assists—for a fat 8 points. I was tagged as a poor playoff performer. Well, that record certainly speaks for itself.

The label stuck with me at Boston as the Bruins finished third, making the playoffs for the first time in nine years. In the opening series we took on the Canadiens, who had finished first. They disposed of us in four games. We faced Gump Worsley, who was to post a goals-against average of 1.88 in the playoffs as the Canadiens won the cup. Needless to say, no one scored much off him.

The next year things changed for me—and the Bruins. It was 1969 and we had more experience. We had tasted defeat in clutch situations and all of us had gained from this. I was supposed to be the biggest stiff around when it came to the clutch. But in 10 playoff games that year I led all scorers with 8 goals and 10 assists for 18 points. Not bad. But we still hadn't won the Cup. That came in 1970, when we won our last 10 cup games in a row and I wound up with a scoring record of 27 playoff points: 13 goals and 14 assists. We suffered a major disappointment in 1971 when we lost in the first round of Cup play to the Canadiens, though I did manage 10 points in the seven games. We faced Ken Dryden in that series, and I've never seen a better playoff performance by a goalie. He won the Smythe award. I had 60 shots in the seven games. Normally, on 60 shots I'd get 10 goals. But I scored only 3.

I think about that last game a lot. The way I look at it, we lost only one game—the seventh. The previous six didn't mean a thing. The whole playoffs for us boiled down to that one stinking game, and we blew it.

That's why I regard the playoffs as a whole new season.

7

Stanley Cup Play

There was no champagne in Madison Square Garden when we won the Cup on May 11, 1972. Some of us figured it was bad luck. Two days before we had had cases of the stuff in our Boston dressing room. Everyone assumed we were going to beat the Rangers that day and win the Stanley Cup. The newspapers were filled with it: "Our B's Clinch Tonight."

We had gotten to the final round by beating the Toronto Maple Leafs in five games. Then St. Louis four straight. After that we won our first two games in Boston against the Rangers and I knew we were going to make it. The only game we had lost in the entire playoffs was one in overtime to the Leafs.

After the first two rounds I was a leading scorer. In nine playoff games I had accumulated 16 points. But the big one was coming up.

We were a little off balance when the playoffs started

93

since we didn't know who we were going to open against —Toronto or Detroit—until the season was practically over. I preferred Detroit because although the Wings had the more explosive scoring with such players as Marcel Dionne, Mickey Redmond, and Red Berenson, their defense and goaltending weren't as good as Toronto's. So I figured we'd outscore them.

Yet we'd also always had difficulty in the Olympia. The Red Wings are tough at home. In fact, most NHL clubs are tough at home. But I'm usually a bit extra tight there because the Soo is only 365 miles from Detroit and it seems about half my home town comes down to see me. They want tickets or autographs or just to say hello and all this makes for a pretty busy time.

Still, I believed Toronto would be more of a challenge. The Maple Leafs had Jacques Plante and Bernie Parent in goal and some strong young defensemen. But more than that, the club was up.

Near the end of the season John McLellan, who had been suffering from ulcers, was replaced by King Clancy; and the Leafs, who'd been going nowhere, began to win for Clancy. There was no doubt he'd have them sky-high for the playoffs. A coaching change can do that sometimes. There's a change in attitude and something electric takes place.

Well, we wound up facing Toronto in the first round. A good playoff team. And the following Leafs particularly impressed me:

Norm Ullman. Five years ago he was the best forechecker in the game. Today he's still tough and pokechecks you constantly. He's got the blade out in front of your feet and it's like dueling with an octopus. Normie is also a goal-scorer. One of the best at deflections. Why he can deflect the puck into the net from 20 feet out. I stay pretty close for my tip-ins, but he's something else. He's able to control some guy's shot while practically on top of the shooter, where the muzzle velocity is tremendous. That's simply wild.

Dave Keon. He's a dangerous skater. His breakaway potential, combined with his alertness and good hockey sense, make him one of the best players in the league. He can kill penalties, and is a real threat on the power play. He's one of the smaller guys who gives me trouble on face-offs.

Ron Ellis. I was surprised he scored only 23 goals during the season. He's very strong, cuts in well, and backchecks hard as hell. When he hits you, you feel it. He's listed at 175 pounds, but teams have a habit of inflating or deflating weights for their own purposes.

Jim Harrison. I've always been impressed with this kid. He's tough and he's smart. I'd like to have him under my wing for a year or so. He's eager to learn. He was Boston property originally and when he came to his first training camp I taught him a trick on the face-off. You push the puck through the other center's legs and then take a shot on net. The goalie's screened. When it works it's beautiful. I'll be damned if he didn't do it to me during a game and score a goal. That's fair enough, I suppose. I learned the trick from Mikita.

Paul Henderson. Hennie is a good hockey player. He skates like the wind and works hard. A solid checker who shoots right-handed but plays the left side, he can really drill the puck from his off wing.

We opened the series at Boston and came away with an easy 5–0 victory. So naturally we figured on a soft time in the second game. But after we got a two-goal lead, we stopped playing. Now why a club does this I can't figure. So the Leafs tied us, forced the game into overtime, and won it. That was a shock to our system. Instead of going into Toronto with a two-game lead, the series was tied at one–all. And Toronto is not one of our favorite places.

What we had to do, however, was crystal clear. We had to score on the power play. In the playoffs, goals are difficult to come by. So when you've got a man advantage you must take control of the situation immediately. In short, success on the power play is essential against such tight defensive clubs as the Leafs.

The power play unit—Orr, Stanfield, Bucyk, McKenzie, and myself—discussed what we had to do to win. Strategy is something we talk over quite a bit on the Bruins. Nothing formal. Just those units which are usually on the ice together, working out problems or trying to remedy another player's difficulty. Denis Dupere and Mike Pelyk had been containing me pretty well inside, where I like to hang around. So we decided that I'd come out more, forcing Dupere and Pelyk to come out with me. This would open things up for my teammates. As it turned out, we got the key goal in that first game at Toronto on the power play. There was a face-off, which I won. I passed to Bobby and he fed Walton. Shakey put it in. The game was a shutout and that was all we needed.

Now we had the advantage. Yet we didn't want to relax. If we lost we were right back where we'd started—all even. We got by in that game, 5–4, and I knew there was no way we were going to lose in Boston. We had a 3–1 edge in games and were returning home.

We beat the Leafs in game five and moved to the second round.

I'd have picked Minnesota to defeat St. Louis in the West and play us in Round 2. But not so. I watched the final game on television and was impressed by Jacques Caron, the Blues' goalie. He was terrific when pressed up close. But he seemed to bobble the far shots. Another thing that caught my eye was how the Blues' defensemen seemed to block most of the shots. Barclay Plager was especially good at this.

We centers—Bailey, Stanfield, and I (Derek wouldn't see much action because of his stomach problems)—talked the situation over and hit on a plan. We knew the defense would go down, so we decided to hesitate a split second before shooting. We'd fake a shot, hoping the defenseman would drop, and then we'd shoot over him or skate around him. We told our lines the same thing: hesitate—then shoot.

Again, there was nothing formal about our meetings. We'd talk over a beer or in a hotel room. I might ask Freddie what he thought of a certain player in a certain face-off situation. Or if I was having trouble with another center I'd ask him to watch me for a period and tell me what I was doing wrong. Bailey, relatively inexperienced at center for us, worried a lot about the other team's centers: how does Garry Unger draw; which wings do I pick up; what habits does so and so have?

St. Louis wasn't as strong a team as the club we'd faced in the 1970 finals. Red Berenson had been traded. Not only was he one hell of a player, but he was also the team leader. Another thing about the 1970 team: Plante and Glenn Hall were in goal. No need to look further if you had them. The current crop of Blues, despite Garry Unger, was leaderless.

We sailed through St. Louis, sweeping the four games by a combined goal total of 23–8. The hesitation shot worked. And the Blues' insistence on using shadows on my line also worked for us. Whenever we went out, the O'Shea brothers, Kevin and Danny, were out too. So was Terry Crisp. All night they just followed us around the rink.

I disagree with this type of one-way hockey, because every player once he reaches the NHL should be able to score as well as backcheck effectively. Coaches waste a guy's scoring talent by making him simply a checker. They tell him to forget everything else. So this single-minded player now passes up scoring opportunities even when they're handed to him. Hockey, after all, is a team sport.

If you watch one line, and put all your best checkers against that line—then another line will score. I just don't believe in checking and scoring lines. Each player should do both.

We had almost a week off before facing the Rangers. I thought the Hawks would have a close series with New York. But they were put away in four straight, and so we started to plan for Emile "The Cat" Francis, the Rangers' coach–general manager. Francis had indicated that he'd put his best player, Walt Tkaczuk, against me. During the regular season he had tried to get Jean Ratelle, their top scorer, on the ice when I was. But Ratty was now out with a broken leg, so Tkaczuk—who had played two super series against Montreal and Chicago—would be hounding me. Tom Johnson asked we what I thought. Did I want to get away from Tkaczuk? I told Tom, "Hell, no. Let's see what happens." I welcomed the challenge. And even if I was bottled up by Tkaczuk, I knew that would mean other Bruins would be free to score. Let the Rangers use their hottest player strictly for defense, that was fine with us.

Of course, we knew Ratelle wouldn't be playing at full strength, if he could play at all, and that we'd have to clear Vic Hadfield away from in front of the net, where he's most dangerous. Cheevers said, "I'll help." And you don't hear that from goalies too often.

Rod Gilbert didn't worry us much, as Don Awrey owns him on his side of the ice. In the 1970 series Billy Speer hit Gilbert a few good checks and he was done for the series. But we knew we'd have to watch both Gilbert and Hadfield to prevent them from getting off those hard slap shots. We discussed the Rangers' trailer tactics—their defensemen follow the forwards in, the forward drops the puck for the trailer at the blue line, and the trailer shoots. Even if the shot is blocked it makes for good rebound opportunities in front. Each of us was to come back hard once New York had an attack on, with someone always picking up the trailer.

It may seem odd, but we preferred Eddie Giacomin in the goal to Gilles Villemure. For although Eddie is usually the All-Star goalie and has led the league in shutouts three times in five years, he's never given us much trouble. Another phenomenon of the game I can't explain. Villemure is simply tougher for us to score against. Both handle the puck well, and we knew if we just dumped the puck in against them they'd act like extra defensemen. They make plays. I told Kenny Hodge that if we face Giacomin, to shoot a couple of high shots at him. This might get Eddie thinking we're going to shoot high on him; and then, maybe, we could slip a few in along the ice.

The night before the series opener we had to be in our hideaway hotel by 6 P.M., where we talked or played chess until bedtime. It's interesting to observe the fellows before a clutch game, as each has his own peculiar habits and particular ways of doing things.

Bobby Orr. He's at the rink by 4:30, when I'm still taking my nap. Damned if I know what he does for those three hours before the game. Bobby is still one of the youngest players on the Bruins, but he handles himself well. He talks a lot in the dressing room. Walks over to each guy, pats him on the pads, and says, "Let's go." About the only really nervous thing I've seen him do is to throw up occasionally. He has one ritual: before each game he grabs Dallas Smith's stick together with his own and swings them a few times. Dallas has the heaviest stick on the club, so it's like an on-deck hitter in baseball hefting two bats. Bobby doesn't talk much after a game. He usually sits around the trainer's room till the reporters have left. He's done his talking on the ice.

Derek Sanderson. I'll miss Derek. He shared the locker next to me and was the most unpredictable guy in the world. You never knew what he'd say. But we enjoyed his sense of fun. Sometimes I wondered whether he knew we had a game on; five minutes before we were set to go out, he'd be sitting there by himself in the trainer's room still undressed. Just relaxing. I could tell when Derek was nervous, because he'd become very meticulous about things. He might even shower before a game. Few of us do that. Once after the second period he started to take off his skates. "What the hell are you doing?" I asked him. "What do you mean, what am I doing?" he said. "The game's not over," I told him. "You're kidding," he replied. But then he went out and got a couple of goals. One other thing about Derek. He keeps a picture of a girl on his locker. And just before he goes out on the ice, he always touches it.

Gerry Cheevers. He was another late dresser. But a goalie has twice as much stuff to put on as a forward. So Gerry was never ready until 10 minutes before the warm-ups. He's always reading the racing forms. He's pretty heavily invested in horses and reads everything he can about them. Every morning Gerry bought *The Racing Forum* and before games he'd usually be tossing things around the room—underwear, shin pads, adhesive tape. The mask with the stitch marks began a couple of years ago when Frosty Foristall, our trainer, asked him, "How many stitches would you have if you didn't wear the mask?" Cheesie then painted them on. Gerry's only superstition was always to wear a black shirt under his gear. We'll certainly miss Gerry, who was always cool as could be. Once after a game we'd lost 10–2 Hap Emms, our general manager then, asked what had happened. "Roses are red,/Violets are blue,/They got 10/And we only got 2," Cheesie replied.

Mike Walton. He got the nickname Shakey because of his well-publicized trips to a psychiatrist. He likes to have five rolls of white tape beside him while he's getting dressed. He doesn't use half of it, but it upsets him if it's not there. He also wants a cup filled with ice water from which he sometimes takes a little sip. Shakey used to room with Cheevers. The first thing he'd do in a hotel room is turn down the bed and hang up Gerry's clothes. If Gerry put his socks on the floor, he'd scold him. A few days after Shakey first joined the team from Toronto, we were at Chicago's O'Hare Airport when Walton lay down in the middle of the terminal. Cheevers immediately sat down beside him with pencil and paper. A psychiatrist taking notes.

Don Awrey. A very quiet guy even though he spends more than a hundred minutes in the penalty box each season and is always popping into the middle of conversations. I call him Bugsie. He knows I'm peculiar about my superstitions and is forever crossing sticks on me.

John McKenzie. Pie will also be missed. He is one of the wildest people I've ever come across. Pie's only superstition was taking the bands off Cheever's goalstick. Otherwise he was a totally relaxed fellow who just took each game as it came.

Carol Vadnais. He doesn't have a tooth in his head. He's got false uppers and lowers. When he's excited he says things like, "Boy, what I got to shoot." I've never figured out what he means.

Fred Stanfield. He sits around so silently before a game that you don't even know he's there. But he's one of the smartest hockey players I've come across. He's got anticipation, a knack for making the right moves. Maybe that's it. Maybe he's thinking while we're all horsing around.

John Bucyk. John wears a cigar in his mouth. Even in the showers. Before a game he's just blah. No emotion, no excitement. Maybe that's why I'm so calm. I sit between Derek and Bucyk. He's always getting presents from some fan or another. Probably cigars. He and Orr and McKenzie and Stanfield had this little ritual. Every game they'd mix up a batch of liniment—to start the blood churning, I suppose—and put it on before they got dressed. Then each of them would shout, "Geez, it's red hot." So naturally we called it Red Hot.

Ken Hodge. His routine doesn't change. He must be the last man off the ice during warm-ups or after a period. Going out on the ice there is also a certain order. He goes before me. Then came the goalies, McKenzie, and Bucyk.

Ace Bailey. You'd never think: here's a guy that hasn't been able to break into the lineup for three years. He never sulks, but instead always tries to keep our spirits soaring. He could have been a regular on any other team. However, this hasn't bothered him—at least so it shows. Maybe that's why he's stayed. He's good to have around.

Tom Johnson. Tom's the one who has to deal with us. We knew he'd be under the gun when he replaced Harry Sinden, who took us to the Stanley Cup in 1970. We're a difficult club to coach because of our talent and kookiness. Yet, I've never seen Tom lose his temper. Oh, he'll find a strong word or two if we blow a lead at home, but he's always in control of himself. Tom allows us our freedom yet still commands our respect. Once on the Coast he said curfew would be at 10 o'clock because our bodies were still on Eastern time. "Come on, Tom," a player called. "Make it 11 o'clock." Tom just smiled and said, "You guys will stay out till 11 anyway."

Funny about the finals. Friends from back home treat it like a vacation. They come to town and think you've got lots of time and tickets. Lou Nanne had people staying as house guests during the playoffs. Though another player, J. P. Parise, converted his five-bedroom apartment to two bedrooms just to avoid people dropping in. He's simply not the type of guy who can say, "I don't have any room." So one bedroom became a library, another was used for sewing, and the third he made into a workroom.

Me? I concentrated on the Rangers. We had beaten them five straight times during the regular season, but the playoffs are different.

Each winner in 1972 was going to get $15,000 apiece. Double other years. The Rangers hadn't won the Cup since 1940 and had a history of choking in the clutch. But we wanted it just as badly as they did. 1971 really got us. We'd finished the season with the greatest record in history. We were favored to take the Cup again. But we didn't. The Canadiens knocked us out in the first round. So we had yet to finish first *and* win the Cup.

I don't know when the modern rivalry between our clubs began. Perhaps it was in the mid-1960's, when Ted Green speared Phil Goyette. Goyette lost his spleen, and Bill Jennings, the Rangers' president, declared a bounty on Ted Green's head. That made Greenie seem like some sort of wild animal. The next game between the teams was expected to be a bloodbath. It wasn't. Which is usually the case. But fans at the old Madison Square Garden were looking for trouble. There were yellow balloons that read "Drop Dead Ted," as well as some pretty obnoxious shouting. The seeds were sown.

Our grudge games continued even when the teams became respectable. Remember that we were probably the two worst clubs in modern history, sharing last place a total of 14 times from 1943 until 1966.

A few years after the Goyette incident, Ted was involved in a rather one-sided fight with Larry Jeffrey. The Ranger had been poking Greenie pretty good all night. Finally, Ted got fed up and unloaded a terrific right. Jeffrey never had a chance. He toppled over and lay there unconscious. Without waiting for the referee to say a word, Ted headed straight for the penalty box. Once again, the New York fans were upset.

The 1970 playoffs, however, really set the scene for our future meetings. That was a rough series from the opening face-off. We knew we could take the Rangers if we hit them. So Bobby Orr rapped Dave Balon a few seconds after the game started; and they began to hear footsteps. A few minutes later Arnie Brown lost the puck behind his net; I got it, and scored. Our intimidation plan was working. By the final period we had built up a 5–1 lead.

Late in the game Brown hooked Sanderson; and soon Derek was fighting with Park and then Fairbairn. Derek plays to the crowd, of course. The fans were absolutely wild. Then Derek gave Fairbairn the choke sign. The crowd loved it. And we socked it to them 8–2.

The second game was much milder. We won 5–3; and things were so tame the crowd kept shouting "We Want Speer!" Billy Speer was one of our young, eager guys and whenever he'd go out someone's head would roll.

We didn't figure to be popular in Ranger town after these two. But we never expected anything like the scene that hit us. Madison Square Garden was the Roman Forum. And the fans were all for coordinating the lions' arrival with our own. The first thing that hit us was the noise and the imaginative signs. Everywhere there were signs: *Pig-Face McKenzie. Don't Talk to the Animals—Kill Them! Derek Is a Hairy Fairy.* Finally, the organist played "Talk to the Animals." He too was a creative fellow.

About a minute after the opening face-off, with the puck at New York's end, Derek's line replaced mine. Just then Ed Giacomin skated over to Derek and said, "We're getting a bonus to take care of you tonight." Derek just stared back and answered, "That's cool, man." But a few seconds later Derek and Balon were fighting, both clubs piled on, and the fans became hysterical. The two were ejected, but not before Derek raised both hands in the peace sign. Sometimes Derek is beautiful.

Well, it took 19 minutes to play the first 91 seconds; the penalty boxes looked like the players' benches; and that first period, with a record of 132 minutes in penalties, took 1 hour and 2 minutes to complete.

From there we went on to win our first Stanley Cup since 1941.

So it was late April, 1972, and we were facing the Rangers again. This time for the championship. The Cup means something, of course. But 1970 was really the big one for us. It was our first and, like the first kiss, you can never quite recapture that feeling.

During the regular season I was matched against Jean Ratelle. That's pretty unusual: two clubs' top lines playing against each other. Usually a coach wants his best against the other team's worst so his best will have a shot at scoring. Except this time the match-ups worked for us because Jean and I neutralized each other. Stop Ratelle's line and you can stop the Rangers. Boston, however, has three lines that can inflict damage. New York's line of Ratelle, Gilbert, and Hadfield had scored 44 percent of their team's goals. While my line, with Ken Hodge and Wayne Cashman at the wings, had scored 35 percent of the Bruins' goals. This superior balance represented scoring depth.

Since Ratelle was just returning after being out two months, I really didn't expect to see much of him. And I was right. Instead, Francis put Walt Tkaczuk on me. Tkaczuk, a strong young player who sticks like glue, was to be my shadow throughout the series.

By putting Tkaczuk on me, Francis played right into our hands. For Tkaczuk was the Rangers' hottest player. So if we neutralized each other Boston had the Rangers beat.

Petty things become particularly annoying during the finals. Requests: "Hey, sign this for my son," or questions: "Are you going to win?" and "Do you have tickets?" That's why we go into hiding. So we went to the Marriott motel in Newton, where we were well-protected. Two private guards in the hallways. No phone calls to our rooms unless they were first cleared through Tom Johnson. And additional security men in the parking lot to keep people away from our cars.

Before the first game, when Orr and I dropped in on Johnson, I learned that I'd probably be killing a lot of penalties because Derek didn't feel right after suffering from colitis. "I want you to stay out of the penalty box," Tom told me. "We're going to need you and Bobby as much as possible. Don't let them suck you into a fight."

A lot of stupid stuff was written about Park's book during the playoffs. I don't think anyone on the club read it, though we'd all seen excerpts in the papers. But what annoyed us most was Vic Hadfield's quote: "The Rangers are unbeatable." Now how could he have said that?

Montreal and Chicago hadn't hit the Rangers, and that's what we planned to do. No one had laid a glove on them for 10 games, and now we'd see if they could take it.

In the first game we jumped off to a 5–1 lead. Then we stood back and watched them pull even, before Ace Bailey won the game for us. I'd picked up three assists. Not a bad day's work. I was getting shots off, but they weren't going in. Still, I'm happy with three assists in any game. Yet later in the locker room a writer asked me if I was angry because I hadn't scored. Hey, what's wrong with three assists? I said. Hodge heard me and shouted across, "You were just lucky, Phil, admit it."

My back was sore. My legs were sore. There were welts all over my body. Tkaczuk had done some job on me, especially in front of the net. And it wasn't only him. Park and Rolfe were knocking me pretty good too. Tkaczuk and I spent some time in the penalty box that game for high-sticking each other. Later, Tom said to me, "Phil, you've got to take it. You've just got to sit back and take it."

That's another sort of pressure you feel in the playoffs. Under normal circumstances you push a guy back who hits you, just to let him know he can't take liberties. It's important to establish this in order to survive in the game.

Our defensemen's shots from the point weren't getting through. I'd been in the slot—an imaginary spot about 15 feet in front of the goalie—as I always am. But the Rangers were double-teaming me and clogging up the middle. Shots that were normally on net were always hitting someone. So I told Bobby that I'd move out a little more, away from the net. This way, he'd be able to get some shots on goal. I knew my effectiveness would be lessened. Because the more centrally placed you are, the better your chances to score. You have more net to shoot at. It's that simple. But we had to loosen things a bit.

In Game Two we won again. At one point I was tripped by Tkaczuk. He went off for a penalty. Bobby could see I was angry. "Remember, just stay away from Tkaczuk," he warned me. So I tried to concentrate on winning face-offs. I had good luck against Tkaczuk. But late in the game with the score tied, Pete Stemkowski came in for the draw. Well, I pulled the string on him, it led to a goal, and we won 2–1. My assist on the play gave me four for the series. And damned if that same writer didn't ask me after the game if I wasn't getting frustrated.

I got nothing except a penalty in the third game. And while I was in the penalty box the Rangers scored. They got three goals right away, each one with a Bruin in the penalty box. The game was in New York; and I heard the yelling. Such niceties as: "You're a disgrace to the Italians," and "Spaghetti head." There was even a sign that read,

"The Godfather will get 7 and 35." I wear number 7, my brother Tony wears number 35. But I don't think the fan was serious. And the Rangers took it anyway.

We won the fourth game, also in New York. Tkaczuk drew me into a second penalty, which we killed; and again, Bobby skated over to say: "Phil, you've got to stay away from him." Still, I'd say Tkaczuk did a good, clean job on me. But he'd get tired, then he'd grab me, and that's when I got annoyed.

People tell me my frustration was showing, though I wasn't aware of it. I'd hit a post and look up to heaven, or I'd throw my arms out as if to say, "What does a guy have to do to get a goal?" Some even thought I was arguing with the referees over calls. Talking yes. But arguing? They just don't let you do that during the playoffs. The referees must keep the game under control and if some player waves his arms or swears, the referee appears to have lost this control. Then he's got the fans on his back. But I'm one of the guys who wears an "A." C stands for captain, the A is for alternate. Only the captain or an alternate is permitted to ask the referee for an interpretation of a penalty. If anyone else questions the referee, he's penalized two minutes. Well, I guess I was talking a lot.

We expected to beat the Rangers in the fifth game, before a Boston crowd, and win the Cup. We were leading in games by 3–1 and for New York to beat us they'd have to take three straight. Home free. A reception was planned at City Hall for the next day. In the press boxes were printed instructions for how the Stanley Cup was to be presented to Johnny Bucyk, and also describing John's victory lap. Down came the champagne as well as some Mateus rosé, but when Tom Johnson saw it arriving before the game he told the deliverymen, "Get that stuff out of here."

A funny thing about that champagne. One giant carton came "from the Mayor's office." Naturally, it was brought inside, the box was opened, and this fan popped out who wanted to see the game. We let him stay.

I'm sure he was as disappointed as we were. We knew we had to hit New York. But we didn't touch them all night. So the Rangers won on two goals in the final period by Bobby Rousseau, a little guy who does nothing when we play our hitting game. Rousseau hadn't scored against us since December, 1969—3½ years. Yet, we let him walk in and score two close ones. We lost 3–2.

Though I'd gotten both assists on our goals, and wasn't concerned about the loss because I knew we'd get them in New York, my old friend came around to ask me if I wasn't upset. I lost my temper. "For crying out loud," I shouted, "isn't there anything else you're interested in except goals, goals, goals."

We had gone five games. I had taken 35 shots without a score. I'd gotten six assists, but no one seemed to care about that. And another thing: Tkaczuk had scored only one goal in the five games, which came when I wasn't even on the ice. I was playing as well as I ever had. I was getting my shots, I was setting up my teammates, I was stopping their best player. During the regular season I might have stayed in the slot a little longer. I was conscious of coming back to play defensively, though, and as soon as I saw the puck changing hands I backchecked. It must have worked, because their "hot man" got only one goal and two assists in the entire series.

The climate of the dressing room before the sixth game was one of quiet confidence. We were in Madison Square Garden, and though it's not the same when you win the Cup away from home, you get a certain satisfaction if you can take it on the road. It shows how really good you are. In effect, you're saying to the other team: "Okay, we're in your territory and we're going to beat you." Bobby was playing gin with McKenzie. Sanderson and Bailey were also playing cards. It must have been Old Maid, because Slap Jack we'd have heard. The rest of us were talking horses and baseball. Cheevers and I were discussing the Preakness. He liked Riva Ridge. Mine was No Le Hace. Then it was Willie Mays to the Mets, and whether he'd become the first black manager in baseball. Of course I checked to see if there were any crossed sticks, and there weren't, so I felt better.

Wayne Hillman got me on that crossed sticks thing in Chicago. We were sitting next to each other and he motioned to a pair of sticks lying across each other. "Watch," he said, "whenever you see crossed sticks in the dressing room we'll lose." We lost.

I put on my black sweatshirt. If you've seen us play, perhaps you've noticed my black collar sticking out. This started the year I got 126 points. I had a cold before one game and asked Frosty Foristall to give me something for it; he gave me a black T-shirt. I wore it backwards to cover my throat. That night I got the hat trick.

I wrapped the blade of my stick with black friction tape. Again, just as I always do. But I don't take the stick on the ice until Frosty applies the powder. He takes a can of Johnson's Baby Powder and dusts the tape with it. The powder keeps the snow from sticking. Between periods we repeat the procedure, I put on fresh tape and Frosty powders it.

So I had powder on my blade, the black shirt was turned backwards, and there were no crossed sticks. I hadn't signed any autographs. Everything was pointing in the right direction. Still there was no noise until we walked through the covered ramp and heard the crowd. Then the adrenalin flowed. We skated through our warm-up and I could tell the guys were really up for the game. Everyone was chattering.

The Rangers started Gilles Villemure; and he was terrific. So was Cheevers. The game was close. We were leading 1–0 going into the final period. There was a face-off near Villemure and I squared off against Tkaczuk. Francis tried to get Stemkowski out instead, figuring that he might do better against me than Tkaczuk, who I'd been beating to the puck regularly. But referee Art Skov waved him back to the bench. I skated over to Bobby. "I'll try to get the puck back to you." "Okay," he said, "but make sure you're in front of the net for the rebound." I won the face-off and laid the puck right on Bobby's stick. He shot, and

Wayne Cashman was there to deflect it home. That made it 2–0. I still wasn't sure. The Rangers were pressing like crazy. Then we had a semi-breakaway. The puck was on my stick and I spotted Hodge with the puck—I really aimed it—he fed Cash, and that was the ball game.

When the final buzzer went off, I felt a tremendous sense of relief. The season had been a long one; and now it was over. We shook hands with the Rangers. Campbell presented Bucyk with the Cup. And Johnny skated a short distance with the Cup high over his head. Short, because a few of New York's more courteous fans had now begun to throw things. And high, partly out of tradition and partly for protection. We left the ice quickly.

There was shouting in the dressing room all right. But it wasn't frenzied. I heard Derek telling one reporter, "Ah, it wasn't any big deal. We knew we'd win. It was nothing like the first one." Typical Derek. No big deal! It was the Stanley Cup! Though if you're not a Canadian it's difficult to realize what those two words mean. It's so tied up with our lives and our country. True, perhaps it wasn't quite as sweet as 1970. Still, this time we'd finished first *and* won the Cup. We were the tops.

We did a little celebrating in the clubhouse, but there wasn't any champagne. Just beer. Some photographers wanted a picture of us drinking champagne from the cup. So we poured some beer into it and tossed a little over ourselves as well. Off in a corner Harry Sinden stood, talking quietly to Derek. Harry had been our coach in 1970 and quit when the season was over. "Too bad you came two years too soon, Harry," Derek told him. "You'd have made twice as much." Then Derek asked me how many points I'd got in all. I told him 24. We had a $10 bet, as he thought he could outscore me. Derek wound up with 3 points but refused to pay. "I made that bet before I got sick," he said. "You welcher," I told him, patting his head. Of course, I'm not the only fellow on the club that Derek owes $10. But maybe with his recent riches we'll all be getting small envelopes in the mail from Philadelphia containing ten dollar bills.

The Cup is only about 10 inches high, as it sits on a base that's two feet. Yet it's really quite beautiful. After the Cup had passed around the locker room for the second time in three years, I was surprised to learn that it's not the original. This stays at the Hockey Hall of Fame in Toronto. It seems that the original cup is made of a nickel alloy which would crack with constant handling. Still as far as I'm concerned, the one I've drunk from twice is the real thing.

We boarded our charter flight back to Boston a little after one o'clock in the morning, had a few drinks on the plane, and were all shouting and laughing and joking. I was especially happy. I'd done well in the playoffs. I had eight assists in the final series, which tied a record. The eight points also tied me with Bobby Orr for most points in the entire playoffs.

But when the plane touched down at Logan Airport, all hell broke loose. More than 10,000 people had showed up to welcome us, and the runways were a swarm. A couple of guys shouted, "Who cares? Let's go see them." So off we all got. What happened then I shall never forget. The terminal building was filled with people. They were on both sides of an aisle about three feet wide. I've had claustrophopia before, but nothing like this.

Bobby and I were together, and the fans were screeching and waving and tugging at us. Before we'd gone three steps my suede coat was torn off and my watch jerked from my wrist. Women were keeling over and getting trampled. One guy started pounding me and I swung my suitcase so I wouldn't go under. God it was hot! Suddenly, it was no longer a celebration. Just then I spotted a side door which Bobby and I headed for. That's the last I saw of him. I started to run and found myself in an Eastern hanger, where some workmen were repairing planes. I jumped over a fence and tried to find the parking lot. Then someone spotted me and shouted, "There's Espo!" and I just ran for my life.

I drove back into town through the Sumner Tunnel. There was no traffic in that direction. But across the center aisle all you could see were cars: their hoods up, smoking. People were sitting on the roofs drinking beer, or leaning against the guard rails. Traffic was at an absolute standstill. Nothing moved. It was right out of a movie, all too incredible to be a part of.

Derek, it turned out, was the only smart one. He'd stayed on the plane for an hour after it landed. Then he switched jackets with an Eastern employee, put on a hat, and got a lift on a service truck. The truck took him outside. He grabbed a cab and took off. No one laid a finger on him.

Before the Mayor's reception the following day, a few

of us wandered out onto the balcony at City Hall that overlooks the square. There were thousands of people below us and, feeling just like the Pope, I began blessing everybody. After lunch, Mayor Kevin White rose to say that there was going to be a special presentation to John McKenzie. We all gave Johnny a big hand. We figured he'd be getting some sort of unsung-hero award since he's so popular. Two years before at our reception he'd spilled a pitcher of beer over the Mayor's head. Now Johnny was walking up to the Mayor, all smiles to receive his award. And the Mayor, all smiles, picked up a pitcher of beer and poured it over Johnny.

8

Getting Ready for the Season

Like most NHL teams, the Bruins hold their training camp in Ontario. Ours is in London, and we play at a place called Treasure Island Gardens. We're based in Boston during the regular season, of course, but find it easier to work out in Canada since so many teams are nearby that it's convenient to schedule exhibition games. Also, every city of any size in Canada seems to have a regulation rink which is available the first week in September when camp opens.

I go to London with the idea that I've got 3½ to 4 weeks to get in shape. And I relax; I don't break my back. I usually report at about 212 pounds and play at 214. But now that I've hit 30, I'm going to try something a little different. Each year I'd like to play one pound lighter than the previous season. This, because it gets harder to carry

119

the weight as you get older. Most of the weight is muscle, not fat, and the muscles lose a bit each year. Training camp isn't an exercise farm. You don't go there to lose weight or gain weight, but to prepare for the season. To get the muscles in tone and your stamina and timing working. Many coaches think that means exercises, which I hate. I get in shape during the exhibition games. The exercises are killers. After the first three or four days even my hair hurts.

The reason we're all so sore is that we're stretching muscles that haven't been used for months. We're twisting and turning and running. And we're doing this on skates. I break in a new pair of shoes each training camp, and hope they last me through the season. I hate to break in shoes during the regular season. They're made of high-quality leather and run more than $70. But they're stiff and uncomfortable when you first put them on. I'll change my blades maybe five or six times during the season, but I'll wear the shoes until they fall apart.

The Bruins run one of the most unusual camps around. That's also true of our practices during the regular season. Sometimes I feel sorry for Tom Johnson, but he must know what he's doing because it works for us. We've always been a loose team. Milt Schmidt likes it that way, and so that's the way Harry Sinden and Tom Johnson have run it. Anyone watching our scrimmages would think we're the most disorganized team going. Guys skate at their own pace, we fool around a lot. Maybe that's why we can turn it on in a game. We haven't stripped our gears.

But that doesn't mean we waltz through camp. We skate from 9:30 to 11 in the morning, then from 1 to 2 in the afternoon. And so the tail drags a bit.

Training camp is not as bad as it used to be when we played 12 games and spent more than a month getting ready. The Players Association has changed that. Now it's a maximum of 10 games, and we get a flat $600 fee for the exhibition season. Previous years players received $100 for every exhibition game against an NHL club but only $25 for other games. Some general managers advised coaches that certain players were seeing too much action against the NHL and so these players were then saved for the $25 games.

Also, starting with the 1972–73 season, all players who participated in 50 games the previous season need only attend camp for 23 days. And the training table has been stopped as well. Some camps had pretty awful food and the players complained. So instead of the training table, each player now receives $12 a day for his meals.

You can be too confident in training camp. Before the 1971–72 season we lost more games than we won. We were cocky, and Tom didn't push us. He figured we'd straighten out. But after we lost our season opener to the Rangers in Boston, Tom got tough. He worked us like crazy the next day. Milt also was angry. He felt too many of us were involved in outside activities. I'll say this: we're one of the most popular home teams in America. And if the guys wanted to they could attend a banquet or a used-car-lot opening every night. And that's what some of us were doing. The money was everywhere, and we were in demand. Of course everyone wasn't in the $1000 an appearance category. But they were getting $250 or $500, and grabbing it. Two or three of those a week and you've a pretty fair extra income. This was disturbing to Boston management when we weren't winning. So Tom called Bobby and me into his office and asked if we'd agree to a ban on outside activities. Since we were the two players most in demand, Tom figured it was necessary to step on us first. We saw the club's point of view, and agreed. Milt then announced a ban on outside doings until the team straightened out.

Two days later we went into Madison Square Garden for our second game of the season and whacked them 6–1. Now, had we suddenly improved because we'd agreed not to run around so much? I don't believe that. I think we were just due to start winning; we were too solid a club to lose. We then won six of our next seven games. Perhaps the ban did kick us off our cans. But who cares? What's important is that we were winners again.

Are today's young hockey players as dedicated to the game as those of ten or fifteen years ago? Or have outside interests so cut into their lives that their attention has been drawn away from the sport? I know this: outside activities don't bother me one bit. Look at my record. I didn't score the 76 goals when I was 25 years old and all I had going was a summer camp. I got those 76 after I became a businessman. Endorsements and commercials and speaking engagements don't appear to have hampered Bobby Hull or

Bobby Orr. Hull was at the peak of his extracurricular interests when he scored 58 goals, his best mark. And Orr was involved in five or six things when he became the first defenseman to get 100 points. During the season I try not even to think about anything except hockey. Sure, I know what's happening to my money. But that's one of the major reasons I've got Fred Sharf. With him running the store, I can direct all my energies toward the game.

I also believe that when an athlete starts to see money on the outside, his incentive to play well is even greater. He knows that the more he produces the more valuable his name will become.

I want my name to mean something when I hang up the skates, so I try to connect myself with quality operations. Take hockey schools. I started with a school at the Soo, and I paid my dues. I pulled about $300 a week out of it, but it took lots of work. I still put in time. When I'm at the school I spend six hours a day on the ice with the kids. If you do the job right, the cost to run a hockey camp in time, labor, and money is tremendous. The trouble with many of these schools is that they advertise players who show up for just a few minutes. Any parent sending a son to such a school should first determine: is it a hockey school? Will the boy receive instruction in hockey or in boating? A lot of schools calling themselves hockey camps offer scuba and horseback riding and sailing. Okay, if that's what you want. But the parent must also learn who the instructors are and whether they'll be there: if there will be three or four instructors on the ice at one time, or just a player dropping the puck and saying, "C'mon, boys."

During the regular season I'm probably closer to the guys than I am to my family. I enjoy the camaraderie that being an athlete affords, the horseplay, the joys and sadnesses, the many good times. I try to establish this with the other players, especially the new guys, in training camp. I ask rookies who are sitting around the locker room looking lost to join us for a beer. If they tell me they don't drink, I say, "Well, you'll never make the NHL until you do."

Once the season begins, every game is supposed to be played at full tilt, as though it's the most important one of the season. You don't know in October what effect a loss will have in March. When we're traveling, I like a roommate. The bachelors may prefer to have their own rooms, but I need someone around to talk to.

Life on the road is so dreary it's no wonder that most teams lose more games than they win. Take Montreal. In the 1971–72 season it had a 29–3 won–lost record at home. On the road, the Canadiens were 17–13. Chicago was 28–3 at home, and 18–14 on the road. Montreal, Chicago, Boston, and New York were the only teams to win more games away from home than they lost. At hotels I want a big double bed, a color television with bedside controls, and a room I can move around in. Imagine if you had to spend three months in a bedroom. You'd want the nicest damned room you could get. It's the same with me. We have 39 road games. And every one of these we spend at least part of the day or night at a motel. Sometimes longer. I'll say this for the Bruins: they order more room service than any club going. We check into a hotel and, boom, there's half a dozen waiters delivering us food.

The key to lasting through the season is simply to pace yourself. We don't work out like madmen, though I hear the Ranger practices are something. Francis puts them through drills like they're ready to storm the palace. New York is always in excellent physical shape. But I believe most players can judge themselves how much work they need and when they should push a little harder at work-outs to keep a sharp edge. A really bad actor will destroy himself with or without someone looking over his shoulder.

Our coaches have always regarded us as individuals, and men. Oh, sometimes Milt will mutter about the length of a player's hair. But they don't try to run our lives or insist that we wear coats and ties. All Tom Johnson tells us is, "Get to the game on time." And we take care of ourselves. None of us walks around in dungarees. True, we've got longer hair than most clubs and dress sportier. But it works. And who's to say today what's correct and proper anyway? I look in the mirror and I can't believe my hair. A few years ago I would have thought it was crazy. And maybe it is. Still, who's to say?

9

A Pair of Blonds

I've played with two of the best—Bobby Hull and Bobby Orr. Hull, who was my Chicago teammate, has the hardest shot and was the strongest and most electrifying skater I've ever seen. I centered for him. We were part of the Hem Line—Hull, Esposito, and Maki. I was never jealous of Bobby. In fact, I was proud to play with him. And today he's the same gracious guy I remember from my first training camp—helping the rookies, standing for an hour after a game to sign autographs, and giving his time to newsmen. Bobby overshadowed everyone on the team. Even when Stan Mikita won the scoring title, Bobby was the great drawing card. Gordie Howe and Jean Beliveau were around when expansion began in 1967, but it was really because of Hull's popularity that expansion was successful.

I never would have been a 76-goal scorer with Chicago, though. Not while I was centering for Bobby anyway.

Every line has a certain chemistry: you need the shooter (Bobby), the passer (me), and the digger to get the puck out from the corners (Maki). My instructions were: when you see Bobby going, give it to him. Billy Reay didn't have to tell me anything else. Bobby did more than play left wing. He'd often switch positions during mid-rush, and I knew that when he scooted toward the middle I had to become the left wing. My last year in Chicago, the 1966–67 season, Bobby became the first man to put 50-goal seasons back to back. I helped set up some of those goals. But the best piece of advice he ever gave me was this: "You can't score unless you shoot that puck on the net. You've got to let it go. If you get off 10 shots, one will go in." That's been my philosophy ever since.

I got to Boston in 1967, Bobby Orr's second year. Already he was the talk of the town, although because of his bad knees he only played 46 games that season. Bruin fans had been hearing about Bobby since he was 14 years old, and he became an instant hero. I still had to prove myself. Luckily, in my first game at Boston Garden I got three goals. It made my year. I had confidence right off the bat; people began looking for me to carry the scoring load, since no one at the time expected many points to come from the defense position. That first year with the Bruins I got 35 goals and lead the league with 49 assists. Despite missing 28 games, Bobby won the Norris Trophy as the league's best defenseman.

Things really busted open my second year with Boston when I got the 126 points. In the public's mind, there still wasn't any "competition" between Bobby and me: I was supposed to be the scorer and he was meant to be the defenseman. Yet suddenly there I was in a scoring race with Orr, of all people. Bobby had set a record the year before with 64 points, the most ever by a defenseman. Still, nobody ever thought Bobby would become a contender for over-all scoring honors. But that's what happened during the 1969–70 season.

He simply got off to one of the most amazing starts any player ever had. And now I began to feel the pressure of losing my scoring championship, even more so than when I was going for the record. The guys started to kid me about it, and I tried to smile. A player would come up and say, "Hey, Phil, Bobby's three points ahead of you." Or I'd hear someone holler from the bench, "Espie passes to Orr— but Orr won't pass it back to Espie."

Nevertheless, Bobby and I got along well. He's a super kid. Of course we were competing, but we were also competing against the rest of the league, not just ourselves. Finally, Bobby and I discussed the scoring race. We agreed that we wouldn't let it change our game. Sometimes you want to show you're so fair that you'll make an extra pass instead of shooting. Anyway we decided to each stick to our style. And I can honestly say that out on the ice I never thought who had the most points.

The same certainly wasn't true during the 1971–72 season when I was battling Ratelle for the title. The scoring leader for each half of the season earns $500, and the runner-up gets $250. The over-all winner takes home $1000.

So if you lead both halves of the year, you get $2000. There's also the prestige in leading both parts of the season. We had finished our half, 39 games, and I had a four-point lead over Ratty. In our 39th game there was a goal that Ken Hodge made against St. Louis which the goal judge missed. The films showed it went in. I'd have had an assist. I thought about it only briefly. I had a pretty good lead over Ratelle and didn't figure it would make any difference. But then the Rangers played their 39th game and Ratelle picked up five points in an 8–0 slaughter of Los Angeles. That gave him first-half honors. As the season went on we remained neck-and-neck for the scoring race. I'd pull ahead by three points, and he'd come right back with a couple. Every day at practice or over the phone, someone would mention what Ratelle did the night before.

Early in March I was leading Ratelle by a couple of points. It was an off-night and a few players had come by the house when a reporter called from New York. "Did you hear that Ratty broke his ankle?" I was asked. "He's out for the season." Well, this sure cut the heat. And one of the Bruins said to me, "Phil, that's great. I'm happy for you." Still, you don't like to win it that way.

Despite the 76 goals in my 152-point season, I'm the first to admit that I don't electrify a crowd. I just don't have the charisma. Maybe it's because I'm not blond, like the two Bobbys. Anyway, that's what I tell them. But actually there are several other reasons. Hull and Orr got the adulation when they were both kids. Orr was winning trophies when he was 19 and got 120 points when he was 20 years old. Hull led the league in goals when he was 20 and scored 50 when he was 22. I was 27 when I had my first 100-point year. They bring the crowd to its feet, no question about that. I just plod along, nice and slow, though I get my goals.

Bobby Hull was once asked by a columnist who'd never seen a game before, "How come the team finished last the year you got 58 goals? Was it because you were selfish?"

Bobby replied, very cool, "I'd suggest you look up the statistics before asking such a question." Bobby knew the figures. Because that same year he also had 49 assists.

One of the most significant columns, however, is the plus and minus column. These figures are carefully guarded by the league, perhaps so as not to embarrass some of us. But the concept is simple enough and here's how it works: you take every player with his team at full strength. For each goal scored by his team while he's on the ice, he receives a plus. For each goal scored by the opposition while he's on the ice, he gets a minus. Thus, if his club scored 200 goals while he was on the ice, and the opposition scored 150, he would be plus 50. If it were the other way around he would be minus 50. Power play goals by either side don't count, although short-handed goals do.

Some players have terrific statistics (shots on goal, percentage of shots scored, winning goals, assists, etc.) but are minus players. That can mean the man isn't doing his job defensively or, just as often, it may depend on other factors: the line he's skating with, who his coach pits him against (some players only face the opposition's best and so will be scored on), and the quality of his own team.

During the 1972 playoffs, while I didn't score against the Rangers, I was on the ice for only one Ranger goal. And that came on a power play, so it didn't count in my plus-and-minus figure. Over-all, I was plus six. Counting power play goals by us, I was on the ice for 11 Boston goals and only one for New York. During the regular season I was plus 55. Those plus figures help when it comes to contract talk—some players might not have had great years for goals and assists. But if they are plus, that becomes a bargaining point. On the other hand, there are guys with 20 goals who are minus. They forget the minus at contract time, but the general manager doesn't.

10

The Press
and the Players

Every player likes to read about himself in the paper, to be heard on radio, and to be seen on television. Because when you have a big game or do something colorful or are having a great season, this attention not only satisfiies your ego, it helps you at contract time. There are some players who haven't really accomplished all that much on the ice, but because they manage to steal the spotlight are able to negotiate better contracts than the quiet guy who just does his job.

Eddie Westfall was never spectacular. He did a solid job year in and year out. Still the newspapermen didn't discover him until we went to the top. Eddie is one of the best penalty-killers in the business. The trouble is that on weak teams good players are frequently overlooked. Nobody noticed the job he was doing. But once the Bruins led the league, and began scrapping to stay there, the newspaper-men began seeing who was killing the penalties. Mostly it was Eddie and Derek. And suddenly he was discovered. Derek, on the other hand, had no such problem.

We all knew what Eddie could do. During the 1970–71 season he got seven short-handed goals for us as well as five game-winning goals. In the 1971–72 season, Eddie scored 18 goals. Again, five were game-winners. Only two guys on the team won more games. But one good thing is that the news media in the States is finally getting onto hockey and beginning to learn something about it; and the more the reporters learn the more they'll write about the fine points in the game that many fans don't yet fully appreciate.

The worst press I've ever received was carved by a Chi-cago writer named Dan Moulton in 1965. It came after we had lost the playoffs in the final round to Montreal. He said the reason we lost was because of Phil Esposito and Moose Vasko. Now that's a bit rough—to be blamed for an entire team's failure.

Canadian writers know almost too much about the game —at least they think they do—and cut up their teams un-mercifully after a loss. You've never seen second-guessing until you've read a story in Toronto or Montreal. It's funny about Montreal. That club has been the most successful in history. Yet even the greatest teams will lose 20 games a year. Still, whenever the Canadiens lose, a scapegoat or villain must be found. Why does there always have to be a reason? Buffalo beat us one night 6–2 and Oakland shut us out the same year. We don't expect to win all 78 games, nor should the fans and press expect us to.

Few Chicago writers—at least when I was with the club —knew much about hockey. In Boston, however, the writers are among the club's biggest fans. They are more than fair to the team, which is certainly one of the reasons we're so loved by our followers. The Bruins have a unique position in Boston. During the early 1960's when the Celtics were winning every basketball championship, the Bruins were finishing last. There was one stretch when they were last for five straight years. Yet, every year the Bruins outdrew the Celtics. Publicity had nothing to do with it. The Celtics were nationally known, while the relatively few fans in America who followed hockey then simply laughed at the Bruins. But in Boston hockey has always come first. As many kids play hockey as baseball. There are rinks and young teams all over the place. Kids even play hockey in the streets.

Few players are friendly in a social way with reporters. I know that I'd think twice before having a beer with one. You're never quite sure if what you're saying is off the record or not, and you're liable to say something that you'd never dream of saying in the locker room. But the guys who cover the team for radio and television are different. They're mostly approved by the club; and you know they'd just as soon keep everyone happy.

I enjoy talking to the press because I remember when no one bothered to ask me a thing. After a game I take time to unwind. That means I'm sitting in my cubicle long

after the other guys have showered; and when you're available, you get asked questions. I don't worry about guarding
my words. I figure if a guy is a professional, he's going to
quote you accurately. But of course there are times when
what you say gets twisted a bit, or hoisted out of context.

Some writers we have fun with. There's one guy, for instance, who always comes up to Cheevers and asks him
to describe the goals that went in against us. Cheesy has
a million excuses for this fellow, and they all sound con-
vincing. I heard him explain once how "the puck came in
and I was screened. Then it hit me in the chest, bounced
off my left shoulder, hit my mask, landed on my right
shoulder and trickled in." Cheevers would have needed an
instant-replay camera to know all that. But the guy wrote
it down while Derek and I looked on in amazement.

When Mikita was once asked to describe a playoff goal,
Stan told the reporter just what he wanted to hear: "I gave
the goalie a left-shoulder fake, twitched my eyes, shook
my head from side to side, dropped my right shoulder, and
jiggled my fanny. Then I scored."

Bobby Orr is just the opposite. In recent years he's
grown uncomfortable with all the questions. And I can
understand that. He's one guy the reporters always want to
talk to after a game. Bobby hides now, going in for a whirl-
pool or a massage for his bad knees, and comes out when
the reporters have left. Bobby's without pretense; and he's
uncomfortable when someone asks him about a big play
or one of his great defensive moves. He's just not sure how
his remarks will sound, so he'd rather say nothing.

Sometimes I feel sorry for the guys who dress in isolation after a game. No reporter approaches them unless they've done something spectacular. Take Dallas Smith. He's an All-Star, and one of the most solid defensemen in the game. But Dallas does his job so efficiently and without any fanfare that few appreciate what he does. He's a traditional defenseman—he lays back, he never gets caught out of position, he won't be fooled. He's essential to the club, especially since he has been teamed with Bobby. One needs a defensive partner like Dallas. If we had two rushing defensemen we'd get caught short. So part of Dallas's problem is that he's always teamed with Bobby. It's tough for anyone to get noticed when Bobby is on the ice. And for his defense partner, I'd say it's almost impossible. After one game, in which Dallas had played his usual solid style, he was dressing alone and the reporters were talking to the goal-scorers, as usual, while waiting for Bobby to come out of the trainer's room. "You see that guy over there," Cheevers announced to the newsmen in a loud voice. "His name is Dallas Smith. He skates for Boston and plays with Bobby Orr. You guys should get to know him." Funny, but until Dallas was teamed with other defensemen during the 1971–72 season, he never got the recognition. Then, suddenly, he made the All-Star game.

11

Out of My League

The revolution in the NHL began with expansion and the rise of the Players Association. Expansion not only gave older players an opportunity to extend their careers, it also gave twice as many youngsters a chance to make the big leagues. Bodies suddenly became more valuable and we loved it. Although all the other sports had their $100,000-a-year-men by 1967, hockey still kept its wages down. With only six clubs and about 100 big-league players, the owners called the shots. That changed. First there was expansion from six to 12 teams. Then in 1970 it went to 14 clubs, then to 16 in 1972. If you wanted good players, you had to pay them. In just three years the average NHL salary jumped from $21,000 to $26,000; the bonuses for juniors to sign went from a few thousand dollars to anywhere from $15,000 to $50,000; and we kept right on loving it.

Even though we became more valuable, things weren't perfect. Players still had to play for the team that owned them because of the reserve, or option clause. When you sign a one-year contract in the NHL it is automatically self-renewing for the following year. When you sign a multi-year contract, the contract becomes automatically valid for the year after it's up. In other words, you always belong to the team.

Then in 1971 we began hearing stories about a new league called the World Hockey Association. And the people behind it came on strong: they were going to get NHL players, they were going to draft the juniors, they were going to get college kids and good European players. Needless to say, we were all curious. But for several months there was little real headway—a new franchise was awarded here, then one dropped out somewhere else. No players were named. The NHL played it very cozy. Campbell welcomed the WHA to professional hockey and said something about being glad the sport is so popular that another league wants to form.

Then the new league held a draft of players from the NHL. Dayton drafted me on the 15th round. I wasn't too insulted at not being a first-round pick. The way these clubs figured it, they'd draft the players they thought they'd have a good shot at signing. Those whom they didn't figure to sign were drafted later for protection. Soon stories began appearing about guys jumping to the WHA. There was talk that Derek would play for Miami for $250,000 a year. Bernie Parent, the Leafs' goalie, went down to Miami and held a press conference announcing that he was leaving Toronto. He was supposed to be getting more than $100,000 a season. Miami soon went out of business, though, because they couldn't get the building finished in time for the 1972–73 season. But a beginning had been made, real money was being offered, and a lot of guys were suddenly very happy.

As for me, the WHA wasn't a factor and didn't attract me. First of all, I was under a four-year contract which I had signed in good faith and was very happy with. Second, despite all the crazy figures being tossed around I didn't really think I'd get any more than I was receiving with Boston. And third, my outside business would suffer. I'm sure the NHL will mean more to people for at least the next few years than the WHA. And when you're selling a product with your name on it, this is important. Somehow, Phil Esposito of the New England Whalers just doesn't sound as good as Phil Esposito of the Boston Bruins. But who's to say what will come.

One of the few people around who took the WHA seriously was Wren Blair, the North Stars' general manager. He began signing his players to new contracts even before the season ended, since he knew the WHA was planning to put a new team in the St. Paul area. It was incredible. Guys who were earning $25,000, and could expect perhaps $3000 or $4000 a year more, were suddenly getting raises of $10,000 or $15,000 to play again for the North Stars. Lou Nanne has an interesting theory. He says that if he were Alan Eagleson, he'd take 30 key players in the league and say, "Okay, let's jump." This way, figures Lou, you get the WHA off the ground with a nucleus of talent and create at least 200 more jobs for hockey players.

I thought this jumping talk was great. After all, what

other wedge does a player really have? For the first time he could get the owners into a bidding war for his services, just like the American Football League and the American Basketball Association. Not only can the pros benefit from the WHA, but so will the juniors coming out of Canada. They're not under contract to anybody. Before the WHA came along, they'd sign with the NHL team that drafted them. If they didn't, they couldn't play. A kid has to be crazy today not to talk to both leagues. All the good juniors will be drafted by the NHL and the WHA. If the offers are equally good the kids will probably go to the NHL. But if the WHA offers more, the juniors will probably take it. A kid who's really good, what's he got to worry about? If the WHA folds or if a club gets in financial difficulty, he'll always find a job. I've never heard of any top player not being able to compete because the club doesn't like the way he talks contract.

The sports world was set on its ear when the WHA announced it had gotten Bobby Hull for a $1 million cash bonus. When I learned that, the first thing I said was, "A million dollars? Oy vay." It seemed absolutely impossible. Yet, that's what happened. Bobby got a certified check from the league's properties' division (which is in charge of endorsements and such) on signing for the Winnipeg Jets. The 12 teams in the new league wanted Bobby so much that they each chipped in to make the million. Some clubs put up $80,000 and some put up $100,000. The important thing was that they landed him. Bobby got much more than the bonus, though. He signed a 10-year deal that in all was worth more than $2.75 million. I'm happy for him. Who can blame a player of his stature? He's paid his dues to hockey and now was responsible to himself and his family for the best deal he could get. Lots of people thought the WHA was all talk. But that million showed them.

Bobby's over-all deal works something like this. He'll be player–coach for five years at an annual salary of $250,000 a year. Then for the next five he'll coach, or hold some other front-office position, for $100,000 a year. However, if he wants to be player–coach for more than five years, he receives $250,000 each of those years, too. Bobby became the world's highest-salaried athlete, and what made it all especially nice was that it happened to a deserving hockey player. But that was just the beginning.

A fellow named Billy Harris, considered the top junior in Canada, was drafted by the New York Islanders, one of the NHL's two new expansion teams. He was also drafted by the New York Raiders of the WHA. The Raiders, who were more intent on signing established players for smaller salaries, then sold his rights to the Philadelphia Blazers, another WHA club. Harris is supposed to be a sensational player, a big left-handed shot who plays right wing. He was still untried. But he'd come along at the perfect time. The Blazers offered him, incredibly, a $750,000 deal for five years. That would have made him one of the highest-paid players in the sport—without even a single game of minor-league experience. The only catch was that this money was to be spread out over a period of 15 to 20 years. And Alan Eagleson, Harris's lawyer, likes it up front. So Harris took the Islanders' offer at less money. Though he still became the most expensive rookie in history—$100,000 a year for three years. That was almost 10 times more than I received. So the Blazers lost out on Harris, but they did wind up with Parent after aquiring his rights from Miami.

The talk of jumping leagues was now more than just talk. Even players who had no intention of crossing over received enormous benefits. There is a fellow named Mike Robitaille on Buffalo. He jumped to the Raiders at more than double his salary—then jumped right back. Bill Flett of the Flyers turned down his club's offer of $30,000 a year to hop to the Raiders who offered him $55,000. Then he also hopped back to Philadelphia. Bill White of the Black Hawks went from $40,000 to $90,000 a year.

A lawyer friend told me: "It's unbelievable. Why, there isn't one decent player in the NHL who won't double his salary for the 1972 season." And that was pretty close to the truth, except for players who were already under contract.

The WHA talked to loads of good men, and made offers to some that they simply couldn't refuse. Pie McKenzie became player–coach of the Blazers at $100,000 a year. At first Cheevers said he wasn't interested in leaving the Bruins, but he was offered $1 million for six years and how could he turn it down? Gerry left us. So did Ted Green, who went to the New England Whalers. Vadnais was wooed by Les Nordiques of Quebec, who were trying to put out a predominantly French-Canadian team.

Now most of these guys aren't expansion players. They're solid regulars with even a few full-fledged stars among them. All the WHA needs is money to get started and to pay the salaries. It will attract fans all right. But fans want heroes, especially in cities that don't know too much about hockey. So the league has to buy a few. If the WHA is smart, however, it won't make the same mistake as many of our expansion clubs did. They drafted players who were in their final years just to put out a representative team. After one or two years, though, where were they? Right back at the beginning. You've simply got to sow a team with young players even though it means you're not going to win for a while.

Recently there's been a great deal of talk about the Russians. For years fans have wondered how it would be if the top pros—the NHL—took on the top amateurs, the Russians. But, actually, we're not that curious about it. It's the kind of game that appeals more to the press and public than the players involved.

I believe a more interesting game would be to have the European champions—who are usually the Russians—play the Stanley Cup winner for the world title. Put the Boston Bruins against the Russians and you'll really see something. We'd know each other's styles and habits and wouldn't have to waste time learning them.

International rules are simple enough. They're practically the same as ours, with two big differences. When a goal is scored during a power play, the offending team's penalized player doesn't automatically return to the game. He must wait until his penalty is over. And you can't ice the puck if you're a man short, as you can in the pros. The hitting rules also used to be different, but now in international competition you can check all over the ice. Though in American college hockey you can still check only in the defending or neutral zone.

Despite the present checking rules, Europeans don't like to hit—or be hit. Most of them grew up under the old regulations and they're just not used to it. The Rangers once had a player named Ulf Sterner. He came from Sweden and was supposed to be a sensation. Sterner had never been checked crossing the blue line, and now he's back in Sweden.

I'd like to see a challenge for the Stanley Cup. If we're the best in the world then what have we got to worry about? Baseball, basketball, and football champions call themselves the world's best, but outside the United States no country makes a big national deal over these sports, so there's no one around to challenge the pros. Actually, the Stanley Cup is open to challenge every year by any hockey league champion. No one ever bothers because they know they're not as good as the NHL. Since the Cup was taken over by the league in 1926, only one team has challenged for the trophy. That came in 1948 when the Cleveland Barons, the best team in the minors, asked to play the NHL champions. But their request was rejected because the league didn't feel the Barons could make a good series of it. The Cup has two trustees who supposedly rule on challenges. I wonder what decision they'll make when the WHA approaches them.

The league is very sensitive about the Cup and doesn't want it won on a fluke by a bad team. That's why the playoff format was changed. When we defeated the St. Louis Blues to win the Cup in 1970, it marked the third consecutive year that the final series was taken in four straight games. Each year the Blues, an expansion team, had been the runners-up. And the reason they got to the finals was because their only competition in the first two rounds were other West Division expansion teams. The East Division finalist got to the last round by knocking off the best. Of course the winner doesn't care who he plays for the Cup; but since the league wants the Cup to mean good, close competition, they changed the playoff format. After one round in their own division, the winners now cross over, playing clubs in the other division. That quickly knocks out the poorer teams. The finalists in 1971 were Chicago and Montreal, and in 1972 it was Boston and New York. No one can complain about those match-ups.

12

The Opposition

There's no way to assess an opponent short of playing against him. Take Andre Boudrias, for instance. He's 5'8", weighs about 165, and knocked around the minors for five years until he got a regular job with expansion. He gives me trouble on face-offs. Maybe it's because he's small and closer to the ice. I'm not sure why, but smaller players are trouble for me.

On the bench we're always rating the opposition. Not just their shooting and skating, but their fighting as well. We know which guys won't take their gloves off and which ones hang onto their sticks. We appreciate the good moves of an opponent and try to learn something from them. It's important to know your opponent, and there are several key factors I look for when I'm up against a player—particularly a center or a goalie—for the first time:

Center. I try to spot how good the guy is on face-offs. Does he give you a big deke or does he just put his stick down and flail away? I've had good luck against the bigger guys. Like Beliveau. Ratelle and I split the face-offs about 50–50. Second, I'll look to see if he's smart. The smart ones are players like Mikita, Beliveau, and Ratelle. They know the game. They know where their wingers are. When you're up against a smart center, you've got to figure ways to stop him from getting the puck to his wings. I look at how he lays a pass on his wing's stick; the way he picks up rebounds in front of the net; and whether he helps his defensemen when the puck's in his own end. I want to know my chances of scoring against him. Will he let me camp in front of his goalie? Sure, skating and shooting are important. But they're less important for a center who's intelligent.

Wings. Speed is the first quality I look for in wings. From a standing start can he take off and break? A fast wing needs a good centerman. Many a quick wing is handicapped because his center can't keep up with him or spot him with a long pass. You've got to be able to lead a player with a pass, just as a quarterback does. Timing is essential. I'm also interested in how a wing works in the corner. Does he dig the puck out? Can he take contact or will he give up the puck when he hears footsteps? I've had two outstanding wings at Boston—Wayne Cashman on the left and Ken Hodge on the right—and we own the record for most points by a line in a season. The three of us work perfectly together. If you've got a digger, a passer, and a scorer then you've got quite a combination. But Cashman not only digs, he's a consistent 20-goal man. Hodgey and I do a bit of scoring as well. So there's three men on the line who can put the puck in the net.

Defensemen. A defenseman must be able to headman the puck. That means to bring the puck forward. I'm very interested in watching how they pass or carry the puck out of their zone. If I spot a certain habit or weakness—say a guy always tends to go up one side of the ice—I'll pinch him off. There are times when it pays to take a calculated risk. You do this only, however, when you're pretty certain you know what the other guy is up to. I also look at a defenseman's ability to block shots. Does he go down at the right time? Some fellows are forever falling and missing the puck. So I know I can get off a shot with them in front of me. Others have outstanding reflexes and seem to block every one. Is the defenseman able to handle guys in front of the net? That's where I like to spend time. Some fellows still have a tendency to play the puck in front of the net instead of the body. That's when I know I can muscle my way in front of the cage and wait for a rebound or a pass or a deflection. But defensemen seem to be getting away from just playing the puck these days. Almost all of them now go after the body.

Goalies. Today a goalie must be an outstanding skater. When I was growing up the boy who went into the net was usually the poorest skater. You'd always see him hanging on the goalposts for support. I suppose that's how many players became goalies—they just weren't able to skate and handle the puck. But the game is too fast now and too attack-oriented for a goalie not to be at home on his feet.

Only a few years ago Jacques Plante became the first goalie to leave his cage and make passes to his players from behind the net. Today, however, they all do it. A goalie must have good balance and quick reflexes. He must be able to think. I study a man's moves under pressure. Is he clearing the puck in the right direction, anticipating the next play? Or does he bat the puck out in front of him and create a dangerous situation. I notice the way he marks off the angles, making it difficult for a shooter to see the net. I study all these things; but when I'm in front of the goalie I just shoot the puck.

These are the key qualities I watch for from the bench. And I've played with and against some of the best. Take Mikita. He's heady and smart. He's not very big and in the last few years he's been slowed down by a bad back. Stan has great wrists which allow him to get off a shot from almost anywhere. He doesn't need much room to shoot or to pass because he has such excellent stick control.

Ratelle is also quick to get rid of the puck. He's very smooth and has deceptive speed. He doesn't appear to be straining, but suddenly he's gone.

Bobby Hull has it all over us in strength. He's an absolute power. I've seen him score from 90 feet when he's just trying to get off the ice. I think Bobby takes more long shots than any other forward in hockey, yet his scoring percentage is always around 12 percent. When you consider that the leading percentage shooters—who do about

20 percent—take most of their shots from close range, then you can appreciate just how hard his shot is.

Hadfield surprised me. I always thought he was simply a hard nosed player who went up and down his wing. If someone had told me a few years ago that he'd score 50 goals a season, I'd have said, never. But Hadfield has learned that in front of the net is where it's at. He's got good timing and knows when to break toward the cage.

Johnny Bucyk is another who seems to improve with age. A veteran since 1955 with never more than 31 goals a season, he got 51 during the 1970–71 campaign. That year Johnny led the league in scoring percentage with 22.6. He seldom misses in front of the net and breaks well.

The goalies are all different. Each has certain qualities. There's nothing you can generalize on. What works for one often doesn't for another. My brother Tony, for example, isn't a stand-up goalie. But he plays the angles as well as anyone in the game. Tony's also got exceptionally quick hands, so even when he's down he makes tremendous saves. Whenever the team loses, however, he thinks it's his fault and that's wrong.

Ed Giacomin handles the puck well. He does it better than anyone. He's a third defenseman behind the net. He used to be a stand-up goalie, though now he goes down quite a bit. Why, I don't know.

Ken Dryden of the Canadiens can also move the puck; but his strength is catching it. He's got this huge glove and he tries to snag everything. Dryden also covers a lot of net because of his size. I got three goals against him—along with seven assists—in the 1971 playoffs, but I must have taken 60 shots. I should have had 10 goals but he was filling every corner of the net. Dryden is 6′4″, so I should have better luck against Gump Worseley, who's only 5′7″. Yet that's not the way it works. Gump has always been the toughest man for me to score against. Again, I've no idea why.

13

Playing the Game

Although there are more rinks in the United States than in Canada, I've played against only Canadians for years. It's strange, isn't it, that in a country of 200-million people, with more facilities for skating than ever possible in a country of 20-million, not one player made it to the big time? At least no one of any consequence. But late in the 1960's this began to change. You'd start to see simultaneously two, three, even four players from the States in the NHL. Now with the WHA signing college players and looking for talent, the Americans will come.

The basic reasons they haven't made it until now are quite simple: coaching and experience. Despite the number of rinks in the country, the number of boys in organized hockey was never significant. Sure there were a few solid leagues in New England and Minnesota, but the rest of the country just skated around to organ music. Even high schools with hockey teams (which were a rarity) played only 20 or so games a year, while the juniors in Canada played more than 60. So American kids didn't get the experience. Up to the age of 13 or 14 they might have been just as good as the kids in Canada. But that's when youngsters at home go into the junior ranks—and leave their American counterparts far behind.

There have been junior leagues in the States, but only in the last few years have they produced players comparable to the Canadians. This isn't a rap at American boys. It's simply an appraisal of their difficulties. Take New York, the biggest metropolitan area in North America. Until 1972, when a boy named Chris Ahrens from Long Island was drafted by the North Stars, not one New Yorker had ever been pursued by the NHL. Then Ahrens, an All-America junior in the States, had to leave New York to continue his hockey in Kitchener, Ontario, where he was assigned to Junior B. "It's like learning the game all over again," he admits. "The Canadians have far more experience and react much quicker."

Dozens of Americans, though, are now getting hockey scholarships from the same colleges which used to be stocked with Canadian boys like Red Berenson, Lou Nanne, Ken Dryden, Keith Magnuson, and my brother Tony.

Most professional coaches once felt there was no substitute for experience, and wouldn't even consider drafting a boy who had left the juniors to go to college. Although American colleges do prepare athletes to go on to the pros in basketball and football, a college hockey team plays only

30 games a year. And that's just not enough action for these youngsters who must compete with kids who've played twice that number of games for at least the previous five years.

There's certainly enough talent in the States, what with all the 6-foot college basketball players who are too short for the pros and all the 190-pound running backs who are too light for the NFL. Maybe now, with expansion and hockey salaries rising the way they are, these kids will consider the NHL. All they must do is develop their hockey skills when they're young, then play, play, play.

I've learned a few things over the years which I try to teach my pupils at hockey school. This doesn't mean that my way is the only way or even, necessarily, the right way —whatever that may be. But these techniques have worked for me and, I modestly believe, are worth attention.

Stopping and Starting. This gives everyone trouble. Most boys come to hockey school with their own favorite way of stopping. But each has a tendency always to stop at the same point in his stride—either off the left foot or the right foot. In other words, an extra step is frequently required. Often, I find these youngsters also veer to the left or right. It's a way they've found to stop which works after a fashion, but it's certainly not ideal. Most people are afraid of falling when they stop; so overcoming this fear is the first step. I do it by having my pupils hold on to the sideboards and slide. They know they won't fall, and this gives them confidence. After a while they slide without holding on.

While they're practicing the slide, they're learning balance and timing. Gradually, I get them to dig their back foot into the ice at an angle to their slide. They hold on while they're learning this technique. And soon they're ready to let go once again. By digging in with the back foot the front foot is free to pivot in another direction.

I like to start by jumping off on my toes. Chico Maki does this better than anyone. A few quick running steps on his toes and he's flying. But starts are best left to the individual to perfect his own technique. Jumping off requires practice; it's a style which doesn't suit everyone.

Holding the Stick. Whenever you're on the ice with a stick in your hands you have the potential to score a goal. That's why you must always hold your stick as though you were taking a shot on net. That way if you look down at your hands you'll see the back of your top hand and the palm of your bottom hand. At school you'll often hear me calling to some boy, "Your stick, your stick." Either he's holding it wrong or he's not keeping it on the ice. The stick should always be on the ice, even when you're skating. Just think about this a bit. If you skate with your stick in the air, what happens when a pass is made? You've got to get your blade down. That requires an extra motion, and takes precious seconds. So always, always keep your stick on the ice not only to catch passes but also to deflect an enemy pass or break up his play.

There's no hard and fast rule on how to hold your stick. It should simply feel comfortable. And don't hold the stick differently on face-offs than at any other time. Why? Because if the puck suddenly comes free, you can't shoot properly.

Stickhandling. One of the most common mistakes a beginner makes is watching the puck on his stick. Even rookies do it until they get nailed once. That brings up the head. If you're looking down you'll miss the play forming. You won't be able to spot your teammates or see the opposition. So you must develop new habits. And the way to do this is by practicing. You skate and skate and skate with the puck until you can feel it there. And after a while you'll learn to glimpse it out of the corner of your eye even when you're looking to the side or in front of you.

When Teddy Green returned to the Bruins after his brain operation he discovered he'd lost this "feel" for the puck. It didn't come naturally to him any more. And when he looked at the puck this reduced his effectiveness. It was especially tough when he had the puck behind his own net with an opponent bearing down on him. Then if you look down to see where it is you'll get creamed. You've got to be able to feel the disk and see the enemy skater to make the proper move. Teddy finally overcame this, but only after hours and hours of work.

One of the safest methods of moving the puck with your stick is the side-to-side carry. Each time you sweep the puck to the side, you raise your stick just enough to clear it so you can bring the puck back on the other side. Two things about taking the puck up ice: first, don't let it get so far ahead of you that you have trouble reaching or controlling it. Second, keep your blade against it as often as possible when there's a man guarding you. This keeps the puck from his view and out of his grasp. I use a "long stick." That is, I keep the puck pretty well out in front of me when I stride and my arms are extended. This style works well for me. I don't know how many thousands of hours I've spent perfecting it. But whatever method you settle on must be refined through countless hours of practice. And this doesn't mean working alone. You need an opponent or opponents. The game I played as a youngster —skating across the ice with a puck and trying to elude a gang of guys attempting to take it away from me—helped me attain my skills.

Shooting. Everyone wants to shoot the puck like Bobby Hull. And because Bobby's slap shot is so dramatic, a whole generation of kids has taken to the ice with one thought in mind—slapping the puck. So they haven't even begun to work on several other shots that are really more useful than the slap shot. This same mania to slap has also held back a lot of pros.

The snap shot or the wrist shot is better. It doesn't take as long to get these off and they're more effective in the long run. Yes, there's a place for the slap shot: if you're at the red line and you want to get off the ice, I see nothing wrong with sending a slapper at the goalie; it'll keep him busy while you're leaving and your replacement is coming on.

In getting off any shot, one of the keys is balance. For example, if you're shooting left-handed you lean into your right leg. I know that in a game you can't always do it the perfect way. You're rushed or you're nervous. That's where practice comes in. If you develop correct habits, you'll find that in most situations you can get off the shot you want. When I say practice, I mean learning to shoot the puck while you're moving. Many players in the big leagues have difficulty getting off this shot.

There's more to the game than just shooting, however. Even the best players are lucky if they can get off six or seven shots during their 25 minutes or so of playing time. The NHL record for most shots in a game is 14. So here are some other aspects of the game that all youngsters should work on:

The Wings. Many players have a bad habit when they're coming down the boards with the puck—if they lose it, they continue skating. They make a big circle and come back to the puck. That's just plain lazy. As soon as a wing loses the puck he should stop immediately and return at once. It's simply a matter of hustle. Beginners often think they've got all the time in the world. But if you're 10 feet away from the puck you might as well be off the ice. The game's so fast that you're out of the play before you realize it.

Wings seem to want to stay close to the boards. Perhaps it's because they feel at home there. I notice that when wings come into the offensive zone carrying the puck, many of them don't cut toward the goal. Instead, they carry the puck into the corner and shoot. I try to tell my boys that when you shoot from the corner you've got hardly any angle at all, and it's practically impossible to score. Mike Walton had this trouble when he switched from center to wing. We were always yelling at him from the bench, "cut in, cut in." Because if you take the puck into the corner you're killing the play. Everything stops dead and you've got to set up. Your momentum is lost. Many wings who haven't learned how to shoot in stride do this. A good shot in stride, however, is one of hockey's most effective weapons. It catches the goalie by surprise. The shooter isn't winding up, and so the goalie hasn't set himself for the shot. The Hull brothers are good at this. They take the puck and cut in. Sure, there are times when you'll be picked up by a defenseman. But often you can still get off the shot. So always practice cutting in, and pretty soon you'll find yourself doing it under game conditions.

A wing must also know how to break when he doesn't have the puck. It's not unusual to see beginners just standing around when their linemates have the puck. Inexperienced wings just don't know what to do. This knowing when to break happens only after hours of practice with your center and other wing. Whenever a new line comes together you can expect lots of offside calls. The players simply aren't accustomed to each other's motions and movements. Some believe that calling out to one another is the key. Not me. It's the experience of playing together which counts. I prefer, for example, that my wingmen follow me on the play: that they should always be behind the center. Say Hodge, my right wing, is trailing me. He must know when to break toward the goal. If I'm carrying the puck and I see the two defensemen standing at the blue line, I know I won't be able to stickhandle past them. So that's when Hodge comes in. Since he's trailing, he can get up the momentum to pass me. When he hits the blue line and I'm ready to feed him, he's sailing and no one can stop him.

Some traditionalists still believe that a line ought to move as a unit, with all three players parallel to each other. But I prefer to place my wings behind me, thus enabling us to make quick scoring thrusts at the goal.

Wings have to be pretty quick at backchecking as well. This simply means returning so as to be in position to play defensively once the other guys have the puck. And don't stop when you hit your own blue line either. Often a wing leaves himself out of the play this way. Say you're the left wing and you're playing against the other club's right wing. You're watching him pretty closely. If your defense is standing up pretty well, you may relax, figuring they'll pick him up. That's a bad error. If the other wing is a skater, he'll be gone. This doesn't mean you have to go deep all the time. The situation should dictate your course of action. For instance, if the wing isn't cutting toward the goal, you can relax a bit.

Wings are usually responsible for the other team's point men when the wings are in their own defending zone. Many young wings like to think of themselves as scorers. But not everyone who makes it in hockey can be a 30-goal man. Dozens of successful wings haven't even scored 20. But they've lasted because they've concentrated on other areas of the game, such as playing defensively. If you know what to do when the other team is attacking, the chances are your coach will always find a spot for you on the squad. So if you're in your own zone, harass the other team's point men. Say you're the left wing. That means you're responsible for the opposition's right point. You've got to be between him and the goalie, just about at the top of the face-off circle on your side of the ice. And remember—keep that stick down. By laying slightly back from the point man, you're in good position if he happens to try to break in toward the goal. And if he tries to pass down your alley, you've got your stick already on the ice and can break up the play if you're quick enough. Meanwhile, you're also in position to barrel toward the other goal if the puck is intercepted.

The Center. If any one man can be said to control a game, which at first seems so fast and formless, it's the center. I'm prejudiced, sure. But the center, I believe, is the general. Or should be. Each game starts with a face-off; and during the game there can be as many as 50 face-offs. The centers most often compete for these, although there's no rule that says they must. But since you hope to start a play at this time, you want your alignment to be similar to a line rush. That means the center starts the play and passes to a wing. Because centers have logged the puck so much they are usually the best stickhandlers. That's another good reason for the center being the face-off man. He's accustomed to making quick decisions when he's got the puck at his feet.

You just don't go into a face-off situation willy-nilly. It

may look like a scattershot scramble from the stands. But each time I know what I want to do with the puck. There's some luck on face-offs, of course. But this evens out. I'm sure that over the course of a game the club that controls the face-offs will control the action and win. Yet, most youngsters who come to hockey school don't have any idea how to line up for a face-off. When the center lines up, the right wing should be toward his right and the left wing on his left. Before I even go into the face-off circle, though, I look around the ice to see where my men are deployed, and where the opposition has stationed itself.

Timing, balance, and strength are the keys to face-off control. And timing is the major factor. Strength won't help if you can't react quickly. But if you've got excellent timing, strength will assist you. First, however, you've got to react to the puck. Still, if you're out of position or off balance even timing won't matter. Again, comfort is essential. When you're ready to face-off, the legs should be as wide apart as the shoulders. This is a comfortable stance, from which you can react with the best balance. Young players tend to have their feet either too far apart or too close. If they're too far apart, you can't move your body easily. Stand up and spread your feet without skates. Now try to shift. It feels awkward, doesn't it? Now stand with your knees close together. Bend forward or back. You'll find you haven't balance or strength. But with the knees at shoulders' distance, you have just the right combination of mobility, balance, and strength. Your knees should be bent slightly. Also, choke up a bit on the stick—like a singles hitter in baseball. You get better control that way.

It would be nice if you went into a face-off circle and the puck popped automatically out of the ice. But that's not what happens. The puck is dropped in a very inexact way—because it's done by a person, not a machine. Yet this can provide opportunities for a thinking center, since each official drops the puck just a little bit differently. So always study the mannerisms of the man dropping the puck. One ref used to look to his left. At that instant I knew he'd drop the puck—and he did. Though I only discovered this after many face-offs. He'd look to his left, and then he'd let it go. Everyone has his own particular characteristics that signal he's about to drop the puck. You must be a careful watcher, even when you're not on the ice. Study the officials.

Once the puck is dropped, a small war is on. And you try to strike the instant it touches the ice. If your opponent is a man with a stick as quick as yours, then you want to tie him up. Strength comes into play here. Say you want to hit the puck to your left. You bat the other center's stick to his left. That puts his stick on the opposite side of where you want the puck to go and gives you a clean shot at the puck, if you're successful. But what if you're fishing for it, and can't quite control it? That's when you use your body. Try to get yourself between your man and the puck. You'll see physical contact between opposing centers most often when there's a power play. The team with the extra man merely has to tie up the other center. Someone is then free to come along for the loose puck.

During actual play the center is luckier than most. He can roam the ice. It's a fatal mistake for him to stand still in his own zone. If a wing is having difficulty along the boards, go help him out. It's the same in the attacking zone. If a center is simply standing in the slot when one of his wings has the puck in a crowd in the corner, that puck won't do the center any good there. So he should go in and try to get the disk out to his free wing. Some clubs send in a wing and a center every time the puck is in the corner. I've been lucky on the Bruins. Hodge and Cashman are terrific in the corners, so I've been able to get off most of my shots from the slot. Still, there are times when you must help out. But when the puck is lost, come back as quickly as possible. Now it's you who becomes the harasser, trying to prevent the attacking team from bringing the puck out of their end. It's here that a long stick helps to knock the puck away. And, remember, that long stick should be on the ice at all times.

The Defense. Let's face it, there's only one Bobby Orr. But since Bobby came into the league he's given a new dimension to defense—he can score like mad. Youngsters used to shy away from playing defense because defensemen didn't get the recognition. They didn't score goals and that meant their names weren't in the papers. In fact, the only time you'd hear about the rear guard was when one allowed an opponent to get around him. Now even defensemen want to score all the time. They forget they're not Orr and, consequently, they forget that a defenseman's first job is, most simply, to defend. Traditionally, that means you lay back when your team's attacking to protect your goalie. Most good defensemen don't expect to see their names in headlines very often. Still they get satisfaction from knowing they've done their job well and that their teammates respect them for it. A defenseman, however, is not going to make the team unless he gets a few fundamentals down pat and rids himself of certain bad habits.

I notice, for example, that most boys have a tendency to look at the puck when an opponent is skating in on them. Now, just as it's essential for the player with the puck not to be staring at it, it's of equal importance for the defender not to be watching the puck either. A defenseman should concentrate on an opponent's body at belt level—not his skates, not his eyes, not the puck. If you look at his feet or the puck you see a lot of movement, but it's easy for him to deke you. Nor will the man's eyes tell you anything, because the easiest thing in the world is to look one way and skate another. So watch your opponent's waist.

The physical aspects of defense are just as important as cute stickhandling. Players have lasted 10 years in the NHL who can play the body but aren't much good with the puck. Always remember that you must take the man in front of the net out of the play. Harass him. Keep after him. Don't let him get his shots off.

Another fault inexperienced defensemen have is their inability, or seeming unwillingness, to ride a player into the boards. No man should beat you along the sides. If you're backing up and the puck-carrier is bearing down on you, station yourself so that he's forced to the outside and along the boards. This cuts down his attacking angle and gives you a shot at him. Of course you can't always manage this, because you must let the puck-carrier make the first move—no matter how tempting it is to come up and meet him. Then play his body. Don't worry about the puck; let the goalie do that.

Young defensemen have another bad habit: they back up too far. There's a point at which you've got to stand, even though the puck-carrier is making all sorts of moves and fakes, and by standing at the blue line you're forcing the attackers to make the first move. Try to stop the opposition as far out as possible. Whenever you back up inside your own blue line, the shooter is just that much closer to your goal. The first time you see a player barrelling down on you, your tendency will be to back up or to play the puck. But once you've hit the guy, you'll develop a little confidence and be bolder the next time. Hitting someone isn't a natural act. But neither is skating.

I haven't said much about shooting for defensemen. And shooting is what all beginners are most anxious to do. A defenseman with a good shot is a tremendous asset to the team. Half the time the defense is in a semi-attacking position: they're at the points when the puck is in the offensive zone. Many young defensemen think their main job is to stand on the opponent's blue line and fire darts at the goalie. This leads to many a crucial mistake. An inexperienced defenseman is at the point and the puck comes to him. He puts his head down—and slaps the puck. He's not even looking at what's happening. But if you just put your head down and shoot, the opposition's defense comes out, blocks the shot, and has a breakaway. You're caught flat-footed. One reason young defensemen are so quick to shoot is that they're nervous with the puck at their feet. They're not accustomed to noticing how their players are lined up. So rather than make a bad play or lose the puck, they get rid of it. If they have the opportunity to shoot, I try teaching them simply to lay the puck in. This gives a forward a chance at a tip-in, or an opportunity to stop the puck and pass it to another player. I also insist that they first look to see if there's a free man. They must get in the habit of catching the puck without staring at it, then looking around. A shot from the point has its value. If it's hard and low, it can lead to a rebound because the goalie will just bat it to the side. If it's high, the goalie may catch it, and that means a face-off at their end. Though, for the most part, a defenseman's best shot is simply to lay the puck in.

Goaltending. When I was a kid the goalie was always the worst skater or the fattest boy. Not today. Conditioning is enormously important. Since 1965, the Vezina Trophy has been shared by two goalies from the same team—except the year Tony won it. It's just too tough now for any goaltender to play every game. But even with the two-goalie system there's no rest. One's reflexes get dull if you're not playing; so you must practice constantly. Goalies must be super-athletes. Not only does travel and the longer schedule take a toll, but they're under increased pressure in the nets. The slap shot and curved stick did that.

Young goalies have two major faults: they don't keep their sticks on the ice and they don't have good balance. Again, it probably comes down to confidence. A goalie feels more comfortable at first with his stick aloft, ready to bat away anything. It's like having an extended reach. Yet the stick belongs on the ice. Why are young goalies also stiff-kneed? They should be comfortable, but when a shot is taken they stiffen—instead of just relaxing and catching it.

Many youngsters worry about style. Tony says, "Who cares what you look like as long as you stop the puck?" I agree. Tony isn't exactly fluid, and neither is Ken Dryden or Gerry Cheevers. Each goalie has his own rules. Jacques Plante insists that you should stand up. It works for him, and that's fine. But the important thing is to stop the puck. And whatever style manages to do that can't be all wrong.

Naturally there are guidelines. You don't just stop a shot and let it go at that. There are the clearing and stick-handling aspects of the position, as well as a certain number of proven techniques which help goalies halt shots no matter what their style. Perhaps the most important part of goaltending is playing the angles and giving the shooter as little open net as possible.

My young goalies are taught to move toward the side from which the shooter is approaching. This way he's protecting the near side, which is the closest part of the net to the shooter—and the easiest for him. This leaves open only the more difficult (for him) far side. I like my pupils to line up with the middle of their body facing the puck.

If the shooter moves, you move slightly toward the side he's moving, always giving him less "near side" than far side. Make him work for his shot. Of course if he comes straight on, you must move straight out. Only practice, however, will teach you when to do this and how far out to go.

14

That Old Gang of Mine

The summer of '72 was one of hockey's most difficult times. The World Association came along and, like practically every other player in the National League, I welcomed it. The owners and management didn't feel quite the same way. I was stunned when Bobby Hull took his $1 million in cash. I wasn't surprised he'd take it, just shocked at the amount and sorry to see him leave. But I was near disbelief when Derek was offered a $2.5 million deal with the Philadelphia Blazers and was gone. As for Pie taking his player–coach job with the Blazers for $100,-000 a season—well, who could blame him? He isn't a kid any longer and that's not bad pay. Pie was annoyed the Bruins hadn't protected him in the expansion draft, and that certainly had something to do with his leaving. Teddy Green, I suspect, felt his future with Boston was bleak.

He wasn't used much during the 1971–72 season. Then the New England Whalers offered him a top spot and a new challenge. Teddy was off to prove something important to him. And I wouldn't bet against him. But the player who really surprised me was Cheevers. All summer we'd heard rumors about Derek and Teddy and Pie. But Cheesy kept insisting he wasn't interested in the WHA. Then Nick Mileti of the Cleveland Crusaders made Gerry a super offer: $1 million for six years. And Gerry left too.

Cheesy was the key. Because as good as the other players were for us, you can always replace a skater. Maybe not for a while, but sooner or later those shoes will be filled. You can't, however, replace an outstanding goalie. At one stage during the season Cheevers went unbeaten for 32 straight games. Now that's simply an amazing statistic. It's practically half the season. We knew we could win with Gerry in the nets. In the 40 games he played we lost only five. Of a possible 80 points, we got 62.

Although I was sad about these men leaving, there were humorous sidelights, especially with Derek. He was in his glory. "I'm the highest-paid athlete in the world!" he announced grandly. He was going to love playing in Philadelphia, all right. "It's like 'The Godfather,'" he said. "They made me an offer I couldn't refuse." Derek put on the town, even quoting a line W. C. Fields supposedly said on his deathbed: "On second thought, I'd rather be in Philadelphia." Shortly after the Blazers signed him they brought him to City Hall and about 1000 people showed up. The last time he'd been surrounded by so many Philadelphians was when he jumped into the stands at the Spectrum to fight them.

"There's no way I'm going to leave Boston," Gerry had said during the spring. "I'm not even interested in talking to the WHA." Then Mileti produced $166,666 a year and Cheesy accepted it.

I was home in the Soo when I heard about Derek and Gerry. And I was hurt. It wasn't so much that I blamed them. But I like to be on a winner—and the Bruins were winners. It takes a team to be a winner, 18 or 19 or 20 guys working together. And Derek and Gerry were part of it. A big part. My feelings were mixed. On the one hand I was happy for them and their security. On the other hand I felt something had been taken away.

I'd meet people and they'd say, "The Bruins are finished." I couldn't believe that. Realistically, though, I knew it wouldn't be the same. There's a chemistry in a team that takes time to develop. I was a little concerned after the season that some of the chemistry had been diluted by our success, and I knew I'd be trying 200 percent in training camp to bring back the togetherness we'd lost. Now it'll be like starting all over again. But I'm not unhappy since our prospects look strong. True, we've lost some good men —including Eddie Westfall, who was taken in the draft by Long Island. Yet, we've still got some pretty respectable penalty-killers in Marcotte, Stanfield, Hodge, and myself. Derek and Westfall were sensational. No question. They were the biggest short-handed scoring threats in hockey, maybe the best ever at their job. There will be some line changes now, that's for sure. Our regular defense, on the other hand, hasn't been touched and should be even better with an experienced Vadnais.

You never know what will happen. In the 1968–69 season Hodge, Ron Murphy, and I set a record for most points by a line. A tough act to follow. But two seasons later Cash replaced Ron. We broke the old record by 73 points. So you can never tell.

There's no doubt the WHA is for real. And these raids happen when you've got a bidding war, though hockey's different from the other sports. When the American Football League challenged the National Football League, or when the American Basketball Association was created in competition with the National Basketball Association, rookies were the major beneficiaries. We all read about Joe Namath's $400,000 deal and Lew Alcindor's contract for $1.2 million. These players had come out of college with reputations that stretched across the country. But few Americans follow the top players in Canadian junior hockey —and that's where the future stars come from. The Blazers or the Crusaders or the Whalers wouldn't have made news if they had signed a top-rated junior player, as nobody in the States even knows who they are. So the WHA went after the established stars: Bobby Hull and Derek and Cheesy. Of course it would have been cheaper to sign rookies than to land established players making upwards of $40,000. But the WHA owners no doubt figured they could spread that kind of money around because their franchises cost them practically nothing by today's standards.

A new NHL franchise costs $6 million. And if you infringe on someone else's territory you've got to pay indemnity. The Islanders paid the Rangers $5 million for the right to play in their territory, in addition to the $6 million it had to pay the league. So the Islanders were starting with an $11 million debt. But it only cost a WHA team about $250,000 to get started, including the $100,000 each club contributed to land Bobby Hull. Despite the fact they didn't get any players with their entrance fee, as the NHL expansion teams do, the owners figured they were still ahead. And another thing: if they didn't act immediately, it would be years before they'd be accepted into the NHL. The NHL will expand again in 1974, bringing the league to 18 clubs and it's talking about a 24-team league by the end of the 1970's. That was just too long to wait, especially for Canada.

After the first great expansion in 1967, only one Canadian city—Vancouver—formally applied for an NHL franchise. The Canadian game was being overshadowed by the United States. It's doubtful the older league would have considered another Canadian franchise for two reasons. First, because every new NHL team must have an arena with at least 12,500 seats. And second, because the potential draw from the surrounding area has to be more than a million people. Of course these fans must also be able to pay NHL prices. That excludes practically every city in Canada except for the three already in the league—

Montreal, Toronto, and Vancouver. Quebec and Ottawa have nice stadiums and large populations, but they are civil-service cities and the people are accustomed to cheaper seats. Also, Quebec and Ottawa are prime television markets for the Canadiens and Maple Leafs, and you can bet those clubs didn't want to share their TV revenue. But Quebec, Ottawa, Alberta, and Winnipeg were immediately accepted by the WHA. So one-third of the new major league is now composed of Canadian teams, and Canada is excited about it. Naturally there will be some dilution in the over-all quality of play, but with the passage of time this is just as certain to diminish.

So the Bruins won't be the same team. And there's no doubt we'll be hurting a bit. I was sorry to see the guys go. They were my friends and they were my teammates. But this may pull us all together again. We know we've lost some talent. Still, we're the tops. You'll see.

15

Da, Da Canada!
Nyet, Nyet Soviet!

I felt a curious mixture of pride, nationalism, and wonderment when I learned that Canada's best players were going to meet the Russians in the summer and fall of 1972 in an eight-game series: four in Canada, four in Moscow. But, like most of my NHL colleagues, I was a bit disturbed about the sudden slapdash manner in which everything was decided. Still, it was heresy to say you didn't want to play for your country, even though many of us were worried about injuries. Team Canada was the name of our club, and we knew this wouldn't be any ordinary exhibition series—this one was for a lot of marbles and maybe even would be the forerunner of a Stanley Cup rivalry. To add to our uncertainty, no one at the league level ever really explained how things were to operate. Now, however, I realize that a major reason for this was the WHA.

I'm sorry that politics had to enter into the selection of players.

The games came about at the request of the Russians, who asked Hockey Canada to put together a team of Canadian "nationals" to face them. It didn't matter if the players were pros or amateurs—we just had to be Canadian citizens.

Hockey Canada is an organization part private and part government-financed with the single aim of upgrading hockey in Canada. To do this it has undertaken extensive studies to determine exactly how important hockey is to Canada. The group has no official standing in the sports world. It makes no rules and runs no leagues. Instead, it examines the attitudes of players and people toward the game, together with the game itself. Some of the findings are quite interesting. For example, most of us have always skated in a counter-clockwise direction. Think about the times you've gone to a rink and skated to organ music. You went counter-clockwise. But hockey requires players to go both ways. Yet, Hockey Canada found that most players can't turn in a clockwise direction as easily as they can the other way. The reason? Habit. So Hockey Canada is now making a detailed study on every aspect of the game, using slow-motion television tapes and other modern techniques. Perhaps a few things will change.

Hockey Canada knows its theory, all right. But it wasn't really equipped to field a team of the best players Canada had to offer. And that's where the trouble began. It went to the NHL and asked the league to pick the coach, the players, the trainers, the general manager, plus the training camp. In short, it asked the league to run the show.

At first the league wasn't crazy about the idea. The American clubs in particular disliked the whole concept. They would have to offer up some of their best players with absolutely nothing in it for them. After all, how could Boston benefit by letting Team Canada use Cash or Cheevers or me? Or New York, with Ratelle and Gilbert and Hadfield? No American prestige was at stake, yet these teams were being asked to part with their best players for a series of games that could be rough, might cause injuries, and would benefit only Canada. There was a lot of talking going on: Who would pay the insurance? How would clubs be compensated for the loss of a player? Who would pay a player's salary if he got injured and was finished for the season? There was also another small problem. The games in Canada were to be staged September 2–8; at the end of the month the series would then shift to Moscow. But September is usually when we start our regular training camp. The players, then, would have to begin preparing for the Russians in August, and so would be lost to their own teams for the entire training-camp season. Reluctantly, the owners gave in. The league then consented to run the games—but on its own terms. Only players under contract to NHL clubs could participate. At the time, no one thought that stipulation unusual. After all, if the league was running the show, why shouldn't it choose its own players?

Then Bobby Hull made his jump.

Bobby still assumed he'd play for Team Canada. It was, after all, supposed to be a team of nationals and Bobby is one of the biggest heroes my country has ever had. Even Harry Sinden, who'd been named to coach the club, was under the impression Bobby could play. But it didn't take long for Campbell to put a lid on that. "There's no way Bobby Hull will play against the Russians while we're providing our players for the game," said Campbell. When I heard that, my first reaction was simple: I'd quit the team. I felt the league was being vindictive, and by requiring a man to be under contract to play against the Russians it was simply trying to pressure its players into signing, even though the season was two months away. Camp would start August 14. This is just when many players are still negotiating. But then the league explained why players had to be under contract to play the Russians: Anyone who got injured in the games against the Soviets would be protected just as if he were playing an exhibition against another NHL team. The league insisted that it wasn't trying to use a wedge; it was simply trying to protect its players. Maybe so. But I still felt lousy not having Bobby along. Soon, Cheevers was also off for jumping. Orr was on the team, of course, but that was just a formality. He had had an off-season knee operation and there was little chance he'd see action. The Russians, though, agreed to Orr as an "extra man" if he could play.

I didn't know what to expect when I reported to camp at Maple Leaf Gardens—our training base—in the middle of August. Like practically everyone else I'd dropped things, such as my schools, to attend camp. The money was simply a token—$1000 for the eight games. Now it was up to us to find the pride and the motivation to make it worthwhile.

The team was quite a collection. There were such fellows as Dennis Hull, Mikita, Frank Mahovlich, Dryden, Ellis, Hadfield, Ratelle, Park, Berenson, Dionne, and Cashman. Dryden, Eddie Johnston (replacing Cheesie), and my brother Tony were the goalies. This would be something.

I don't know how it is for other players when they're traded or appear on an all-star team with former enemies, but I've always felt that my teammates were automatically my friends. I've worked hard to be close to the men I play with—either at the Soo or in Chicago or Boston. Toronto was no different.

We felt no sense of impending drama when we, the finest players in the world, got together at the rink. In fact, it seemed sort of old-hat. Harry was back as my coach and he hadn't changed at all. All we did the first day was report for physicals—something we do the first day of every training camp—and attend a short meeting where Harry spoke about procedure. The usual training-camp things, like when the workouts would be. Harry didn't set a curfew. But we'd never had one when he was at Boston either.

Harry told me I'd be playing with Cashman and J. P. Parise of Minnesota. Cash would be my right wing. No sweat as far as I was concerned. Cash had played both wings with me. As for J. P., we're friends from way back. He and I run hockey schools together in Minnesota. Only one line in the entire league would stay together—Ratelle, Gilbert, Hadfield.

The next morning at 8:30 we lined up for exercises. The ice was terrible, and the forecast was for hot, humid weather the rest of the month. I reported at 217 pounds, about five pounds more than I figured to start the season at. I sure could have met that weight after the first calisthenics though.

Luckily, I'd gone to Toronto right from my Minnesota school, where I'd been putting in six hours of ice time a day, because the routine at the Gardens worked something like this: Exercises from 8:30 to 9. Shoot from 9 to 10. Scrimmage from 10 to 11. Then we'd return for an hour in the afternoon.

That's a pretty full schedule; and with Tony as my roommate we didn't leave the game on the ice.

From the beginning, every one of us felt we were the best and they'd have to show us what they could do. In fact, that's what worried me about the whole series: Canada produces the world's best players—I'm sure of it. Professionals only? The Russians are just as professional as we are. They even have an advantage over us. Their all-star team—the national team—plays together ten months a year. They've all got civil service jobs or else they're in the armed forces. Someone pays them to play. It's that simple. So what would these games prove? If we won, everyone would say it was expected. But if we lost, then they'd claim we were over-rated. We couldn't get the best of it no matter what happened. Yet, I must confess, as each day passed I became more and more anxious about the upcoming meeting.

We'd heard lots of stories about the Russians—how they have these crazy drills in front of the net before a game; how they never become tired; how precise their positional play and passing is. On and on. Look, we knew they were good. They win the Olympics or a world championship every time they step on the ice.

Harry didn't talk much about them at first. It was almost as if we were preparing to meet just another team. All he said was to shoot every chance we got because their goaltending wasn't as good as ours. Their goalies never see long shots. It's just not the European style for a shooter to rifle the puck from sixty feet out. I wondered what their goalie might say if Bobby Hull could have blasted one at him. At the Moscow Sports Palace, where the Russian games would be held, there isn't even any protective glass around the rink. It's chicken wire of some sort; and I was afraid this would give us trouble because of the strange bounces the puck might take. But I've seen slapshots rip through wire like a cannonball, so I was concerned for the fans as well. Harry also reminded us about penalties. Under international rules if a player is penalized for fighting he's kicked out of the game. Not only that, but his club is shorthanded for ten minutes—the whole ten minutes, even if the opposition scores. The other major rule difference concerns icing. The team that is down a man can't ice the puck as it's allowed to in the NHL. One other thing: There'd be two referees instead of a referee and two linesmen. This I figured would help me; the extra ref can call penalties, and maybe some of my opponents' holds on me in front of the net would now be detected.

We had just a little over two weeks of training camp to prepare for the Russians. Naturally, they'd been practicing like mad for these games. I was determined not to alter my style. I didn't think about the penalty for fighting. I'd abide by the rules. I would exercise as I always did and prepare myself in just the same manner. Our scrimmages were funny though. There was absolutely no hitting. The Bruins have rougher camps. Here everyone seemed on his best behavior. I don't think the Russian scouts picked up a thing. But there were always a couple of them at each scrimmage, sitting in the stands and taking notes like crazy. I met one. He didn't speak English and my Russian isn't much. So I said "Hi" and shook his hand. My juices were beginning to flow, however. A good sign. Deep inside I felt a healthy spot of enmity developing. I was ready.

There was no secret what this series meant to Canadians. Sinden told us right off: "Canada is first in the world in hockey and wheat. . . . In that order." He also knew, as we did, who stood to benefit. "The Soviets have nothing to lose. If we win it's expected. We're the pros. If we lose, it's a big thing for them." And there it all was again.

Harry worried the rule differences. He didn't like having only two officials. Nor did he care for the international interpretation of boarding which concerned him, especially with fellows like Awrey and Cashman. Explained Harry: "Based on our intra-squad games, the refs call it according to the sound the boards make. If it sounds too loud, they call a penalty."

The papers reported that the Russians liked to goad opponents by spitting at them or delivering an elbow. I also learned something from their number two coach, Boris Kulagin, who runs the workouts under the eye of their number one man, Vsevolod Bobrov. In choosing a team, Kulagin explained, "First, there is physical fitness. Then psychological fitness. Then technical ability. Then courageous play."

There was an element of mystery about the Russians that intrigued us all. For, despite our scouting reports, we really didn't know what to expect. The series was opening smack in the middle of the Olympics and, as usual, Canada wasn't winning a thing. I had to laugh watching one telecast in which a Canadian swimmer finished second. That's all the announcer talked about, almost forgetting that the guy who finished first—from another country —had set a world record.

The hockey games, however, were going to keep us first in the world in at least one big thing. Practically everyone in the country was going to see us. It was estimated that 80 percent of Canada would watch. Canadian TV sponsors were preparing to shell out $27,500 a minute—2½ times the normal TV advertising rate for a hockey game.

Still you couldn't tell there was any excitement from

watching the Russians. They sat at our final tuneups in the Montreal Forum as though watching the late show. A few guys in suits took notes. But the players would just sit there, not even talking among themselves. And they always wore those blue stretch pants and blue warm-up jackets of theirs. They wore them to breakfast. They wore them to lunch. And they wore them to and from the rink.

Even though the Russians had arrived a few days before the first game was scheduled in Montreal, I knew one thing: I didn't want to watch them work out. I've learned over the years that you can't tell a thing about a team from its workouts. If anyone came to a Bruins' practice he'd swear we were a bunch of kooky amateurs. The kookiness is there all right. But we're the best on Boston no matter how we scrimmage.

Of course, everyone didn't feel as I did. Some found the Russian workouts significant. Still, from what I heard, the sessions were a laugh: the Russians wore outmoded helmets; their goalies wore cage masks we hadn't seen since junior days; Russian skates weren't even pro models—they were the second-best skates made. And their sticks! These were a Scandinavian model labeled "Montreal Surprise." The papers were filled with this stuff. My God, you'd have thought we were meeting a bush-league team.

Then the workouts came. The Russians showed nothing. I wasn't surprised to read that these guys couldn't hope to play with us. During practice their defensemen kept backing up. A stickhandler would be given a clear shot at the cage while their goalie just waved at the puck. Now how could the Russians think they'd beat us, the NHL stars, playing like that? Not a chance.

One thing about the Soviets did impress the people who watched them. Their stamina. These guys just skated and skated. No one wiped his face with a towel after a wind sprint. No one bent over to catch his breath. No one sneaked a drink from the plastic bottle. These guys not only were in good shape, they were tough-looking. Not too tall, mind you, but sturdy.

On the day of Game One I was nervous; in fact, I think I was more nervous than before any game I've ever played. There were a bunch of thoughts inside me: Were these Russians such pushovers as our scouting reports led us to believe? Who would they put on me? And then, always, the fact that we were supposed to be the world's best hockey players. Hadn't Canada pulled out of the world championships just a few years before because the international federation prohibited pros on the club? We'd said we wouldn't get back into international play until we could ice our best players. Now Canada was doing just that. This wasn't just a team. It was a cause. At least that's the way things were building. Me? I tried to keep clear of all this. But how does one escape a holy crusade?

We were supposed to have a light skate at the Forum at noon. This would be followed by a team meeting. I got to the rink early and waited around. Standing near our dressing room I could see the Russians from the corner of my eye. Fred Shero, coach of the Flyers, was talking to a reporter: "Look how they shoot off the wrong foot," he was saying. "There's only one way to shoot—and that's the right way." More put-downs of the Russians. Why, though, was I getting so uptight? I asked someone the time. Five minutes past 12. The Russians were supposed to be off the ice. But they continued to skate as if we weren't even around. It was our turn to go out. They were holding us up, holding up our meeting, our lunch, our pre-game nap.

"You see," said Frank Mahovlich, "they'll do anything to psyche us."

I laughed. Psyche, shmyke. Our scouts said that their goalie, a 21-year-old kid named Vladislav Tretiak, couldn't stop a thing, and their shooting was bad. Let them psyche us all they want, I figured. The better team wins on the ice. I'd let my stick do the talking.

When we returned to the Forum that evening I could hear people asking, "Who's got tickets?" They were going for $100 a pair—tickets that cost $7 a piece—and those who were lucky got them in the national lottery.

I was going to be on the starting line, with Yvan Cournoyer and Mahovlich as my wings. I'd have felt more comfortable with Parise and Cash; but Harry knew this first game was important, and he wanted as many all-stars out there as possible. Dryden would be in the nets, although Ken hadn't looked as sharp in the workouts as Tony or Eddie J. Still, I guess Harry figured that Montreal's goalie would be especially "up" for the home fans.

It took thirty seconds for us to score. I won the face-off,

we drove in, big Frank took a shot. I was in the Garden Spot, right near Tretiak; when the rebound came out, I put it in.

Six minutes later we scored again to put us ahead 2–0. But now I began to feel a little funny about the whole thing. Here they were, down 2–zip on strange ice in a foreign country, yet they looked as fresh as when the puck had first been dropped. It must have been 90° in the Forum—Montreal was stifling under a heat wave. I could sense that we just weren't in good condition. And they were.

Before long my fears were realized. They tied the game; then went ahead in the second period with two more scores. A center named Vladimir Petrov, who was assigned to cover me, began to do a job. Still, I was able to get off my shots. I must have had six or seven right on goal, directly at Tretiak. But my timing was off. Three or four should have gotten past him. By the final period we were completely frustrated. We started getting chippy, taking little shots at the Russians. They beat us 7–3.

Like everyone else on the team, I wanted to get off the ice just as soon as possible. The fans cheered the Russians' last three goals, damning us at the same time. When we got into the dressing room we just sagged there. We were humiliated. Suddenly John Ferguson, our assistant coach, hollered at us to get back on the ice, that we were supposed to shake hands with the Russians. Now I'd never played in international competition before and neither had most of the other guys. No one had informed us that it's traditional to shake hands after a game. So we all got out of the dressing room pretty quick. But then John told us to forget it since the Russians had left the ice. Red Berenson and Ken Dryden had had to do the job for us. They'd both played international games before and knew the customs. The rest of us didn't.

The Russians tried to be diplomatic after the victory. Their coach, however, who'd been saying right along that he hoped "to learn" from us, put us down rather neatly. "I hope both clubs benefited from this game," he said. Then he delivered the zinger: "I understand some of your best players weren't available."

The whole country was crushed by the defeat. The players were roaring mad. What the hell had happened? What were all those scouting reports about? Whoever had scouted their goalie had better look for a new job. But time was short. We had a second game two nights later, and we wanted our honor back.

We were dumb that first game. If one team, say, the Rangers or Bruins or Canadiens or Black Hawks, had been selected with five or six pick-ups from other teams, they'd have beat the Russians. Especially if the games were held midseason. But you can't do that. There's no way the American clubs will put their players on the line at the height of the season. These Russians, though, had been working out since July. We'd been together only 2½ weeks, from the middle of August. Sure they were tough. But like Don Awrey said, "They told us what we wanted to believe." They poor-mouthed themselves and we fell for it. Everyone did.

Just a few hours before the first game Hadfield was watching the Russians practice. They were passing as if playing soccer—four, five, six passes and then the shot on goal. Sure they looked sharp with no Awrey or Park out there hounding them. "They'll be lucky if they get off five passes during the game," Vic said.

Well, if only that had been true. Not only was their passing sensational, but they played tough defense too. They used a three-man wedge defense, with one player always back. And that third man returned so fast you'd have thought he was on a bicycle. The result: no breakaways. Someone was always back there ahead of us.

The last man, of course, was their goalie. This Tretiak was supposed to be an Army private. But if he continues to play as he did in the first game, he'll be a general soon. He also did a bit of psyching himself. The day before that game his coach brought him out to a press conference; it was the first time a Soviet player had ever been interviewed. Usually, it's only the coaches. But Tretiak talked for an hour, explaining how he tried to pattern himself after Jacques Plante and Giacomin. You'd think that would mean he'd move around a lot and stickhandle quite a bit, right? Wrong. That first game he never left the crease.

"They're going to be pretty cocky after this," Gilbert said. "Before the game it was country against country.

Now it's us against them." He was miffed because his line had been throttled. Still, he managed a smile. "Hey," he asked, "what's the Canadian equivalent for Siberia?"

We moved on to Toronto the same night, and the next day we really caught it. Page One headlines: "We Lost. Une Leçon. Le Canada Écrasé." I now decided to try a little psychology of my own.

Our next workout we skated first. The Russians would follow us. And since they'd stayed past their allotted time in Montreal, I figured I'd do the same thing. Everyone left the ice, except me and Eddie J. I took some shots at him. But out came the Russians, just as if we weren't there. I stayed for five minutes and was surrounded by them the whole time. Well, so much for my act.

After Eddie and I got off Mahovlich said, "When we get to Moscow let's sleep outside the city in tents. That way they won't be able to psyche us."

Frank kept his sense of humor. He offered one Russian a box of chocolates (refused) while Cash offered another a cigar. "No smoke, no smoke," the Russian kept repeating.

Frank did get annoyed before one skate, however, when a Canadian politico came out to have his picture taken with the Soviets. "Politicians," sneered Frank. "He's posing for pictures and we're going to have to meet their army."

And it was almost like meeting an army. These guys were well-drilled under fire. Their goalie—the one who wasn't meant to stop anything—had been practicing with a Russian machine that duplicates slapshots up to 130 miles an hour. Bobby Hull's slapper at 118 mph was supposed to be the fastest. But Tretiak was working out with this machine, and the coach could aim at the upper left corner or the lower right. The goalie didn't know where it was coming from. That's a pretty good way to practice stopping slapshots. No, sir, these Russians weren't the clowns everyone made them out to be. Sure, they guzzled Cokes. And outside their hotel rooms were cases of Italian mineral water. Mineral water and Cokes, that's all they drank.

But none of this concerned us. Because what you saw of the Russians wasn't what you got. It would take hard work and some different strategy to stop them.

Both Sinden and Ferguson agreed the Soviets were weak in their own zone. Give them some muscle in the corners and we'd get the puck. But hesitate and they're gone. They bring up the puck fast; before you know it they have a 3 on 2 situation, which almost always leads to a shot on goal. So to control the action we decided to dump the puck in and chase it. Maybe we'd give them some muscle too and then pick up the free puck. At least this way we'd be deep in their end, and even if we didn't control play they'd have to work pretty hard to break out on one of their quick rushes.

Harry also switched lines around, dropping Ratelle's completely. That must have been a shock to them. Here they were, the highest scoring line in the NHL only a few months before, and now they were out of a clutch game. Harry put me back with J. P. and Cash. I felt much more comfortable. He also called on Tony to play goal and dropped Dryden. That didn't surprise me. Against the Russians Dryden isn't the same goalie. He'd played them once before this series—on the national team—and gave up 9 goals. That's 16 in two appearances. They had his number.

Petrov was on me again in Game Two. Even when I didn't have the puck he was there, just waiting for me to touch it. And was it ever tough maneuvering through that club! Their wedge defense did this, like trying to bust through Leningrad. No one scored the first period, though I felt we'd get to them eventually. Cash was making the Russians hear footsteps and Harry's changes finally paid off. In the second period Cash collided with Vladimir Lutchenko, one of their best defensemen. Wayne went down with Lutchenko. As Cash got up he stepped on Lutchenko's stick. It snapped like a twig. We began swarming near Tretiak; the Russians had only five sticks to our six, and I put in the goal that gave us a 1–0 lead. We didn't let up this time, though. Our pressing and hitting were making the Russians sloppy. Maybe they were nervous—because now their passes were suddenly winding up on Canadian sticks. And whenever they did get off a shot, Tony was there. He was super. Russia was still tough around the net, but Tony was tougher. We kept the edge to win 4–1.

Cash was happy. We all were. And relieved. We had vindicated ourselves. Harry had us playing a Boston-style game and it was working. Had Cash been talking to the Russians in the corners? "Oh, they'd say a few words and

I'd say a few back," he told me. "I don't know what they were saying—but I think they knew what I was talking about."

Another happy guy was Pete Mahovlich. He'd scored our neatest goal, going around a defenseman and pulling out Tretiak, then shoveling in the puck. Big Pete was tired. We all were. It had taken a total effort.

"I don't know whether I could do that for 78 games," Pete said. "You just can't keep up that pace for a whole season." I wondered, though, whether the Russians did.

Harry was on high. He'd been criticized by a lot of people, including Campbell, for his opening game line-up. Many thought Harry should have picked his team in camp and stayed with it. Guy Lapointe of the Canadiens was upset by Campbell's criticism: "The man's our own president and he's not standing behind us. How does he think that makes us feel?"

Sinden remained quiet after the Montreal disaster. He could easily have blamed the scouting reports, he could have blamed Hockey Canada, he could have blamed the whole set-up that put 35 strangers together for 2½ weeks and suddenly demanded a team of 19 starters.

Harry could talk a little after the victory, though. "Before this started I was just a guy from Rochester with a million friends," he said. "Now I can count them on one hand."

Perhaps our best defenseman during the first two games had been Serge Savard of the Canadiens. But we were all confident as we moved to Winnipeg for the third game.

The new lines had clicked and the defense was getting adjusted to these wild Russian skaters. Our timing was coming back. I was in good shape. It took only one game—Montreal—to get me there. But at Winnipeg Savard got in the way of a shot during scrimmage. That did it. He was out with an injured ankle. Suddenly, I became angry. We were playing all out for our country and many people had begun to criticize us for not trying hard enough. Others were simply angry that we'd lost the first game. But here was Savard working to come back after spending most of his career out with a broken leg, and now he was hurt again.

I wasn't only angry at Team Canada's critics. I was also miffed at two guys who were invited to join us but didn't show up. There's no point in fingering them. They know who they are and the rest of us know who they are. One claimed he'd had an operation after the previous season. Bull. He didn't have any operation. The other said he'd just put up money for a hockey school and wanted to look after his interest. Well, hell, we'd all made sacrifices. And here Savard gets cracked again while these two watch television. They'll have to live with themselves.

We moved pretty good in Game Three. The tactics we'd tried at Toronto were working and by the second period we had a 4–2 lead. Tony was sensational but so was Tretiak. We took 32 shots the first two periods and had the Russians off their game. In the final period, however, we lost Cash. Wayne got a misconduct penalty. Then we lost another bruiser, Guy Lapointe, the Montreal defenseman. He hurt his ankle and left on a stretcher. Our defense was a little ragged. The Russians got two short handed goals, followed by two others from a kid line composed of three players each 21 years old. I felt disjointed. I didn't know who my defensemen were or where they'd be. One minute one pairing was in back of me, and the next, another. The game ended in a 4–4 tie.

Vancouver and Game Four were a nightmare. Fans in the street ridiculed us. The newspapers still couldn't believe what was happening. Here, supposedly, was the best collection of hockey players in the world competing against a bunch of amateurs, and in three games on our own ice we'd only won once. I was confident though. I figured Harry would start Tony again, and my line was moving well.

Maybe it sounds like second-guessing now, but I never expected Harry to start Dryden at Vancouver—which he did. The goalie simply hadn't proved he could handle the Russians. But there was change after change, just when you'd gotten to know who your teammates are and to feel comfortable with them.

Game Four opened with a quiet ceremony, a moment of silence for the Israeli Olympians who'd been killed the day before at Munich. A few minutes later we had a penalty and the Russians scored. Then we got another penalty and they scored again. The fans now started to cheer the Russian goals and, of course, I was furious because their cheering was really directed against us. I knew that and so did everyone else on Team Canada. We were really down. The spirit was gone. Still, we cut their edge to 2–1 and then Gilbert tied the game—only to have the goal disallowed. We took 23 shots at Tretiak in the final period, all to no avail. The Russians won 5–3.

So there it was: four games and only one victory. The defeats hurt. No question. But what was almost as distressing was the fans' reaction. Some seemed positively glad. It wasn't as if we'd been boasting for years about our supremacy. We had all given up something to play in this series, and even though we weren't happy about the ground rules or the time of year, we were playing. Later, on Canada's star-of-the-game show, I told the TV audience how disheartened the players were at the way we'd been ridiculed. By the time I got back to the dressing room there'd been calls from fans all over supporting us. More than 250 telegrams came in before we left Vancouver the next day. And when our plane landed at Toronto there were several thousand people waiting for us, carrying signs that read, *We're With You,* and *Go, Team Canada.* Our spirits were on the mend.

Yet our trial wasn't over. Were we really the best hockey players in the world? Four games remained in the series. But now people began examining our training procedures and our way of life. We were "pampered" and "too wealthy"—simply because the Russians, trained to a peak with players who knew each other, had beaten us. One reporter even suggested that, like the Russians, we should carry our own equipment to the rink. Everyone had an answer.

My own answer was simple. Put them up against a team with experience, against guys who play with each other months on end. Okay, the next Cup champion! These games in Canada didn't prove a thing. Well, maybe one thing: When you're on top, a lot of people are rooting against you. After the boos in Vancouver, Bill Goldsworthy of Minnesota had said, "I'm ashamed to be a Canadian." And I, too, was pretty upset.

The Russians, on the other hand, seemed rather pleased with themselves. "Why, Tretiak isn't even considered our best goalie," one smirked. While Kulagin, their second coach, was now refering to Tretiak as a lieutenant. The week before he'd only been a private. It figured. But who could blame them. "If someone gave them a football," said big Frank, "they'd win the Super Bowl in two years."

Harry's attitude was perhaps the most understandable: "On the basis of the bad information we had for this Russian series, we don't trust anyone any more."

Sure, I knew what hockey fans were thinking after the first four games. My country was stunned. Yet strangely, the guys weren't down on themselves. Maybe it sounds funny to say I was confident, that I knew we'd get the Russians in Moscow. But that's exactly how I felt. When you're in a series like this one you can't allow a bad game or two to overwhelm you. If that happens, you're gone.

Our European schedule called for two games in Sweden, to get accustomed to the wider ice surface, and then Moscow. I was beginning to feel better about the Canadian reaction to our team—maybe my little speech on television had something to do with it. In any event, as we prepared to leave for Stockholm, there was no question: the country was united. Almost as if it was sending over troops to fight for Canadian glory. Which, by the way, was what this whole thing was turning into.

But first we met the Swedes. Probably the dirtiest, sneakiest players I've ever run across. Spearing, hooking, kicking—you name it, they did it. We weren't exactly in the best humor anyway, and then we had to play these guys. That first game in Sweden we also came up against a pair of West German referees named Baader and Kompalla. Well, I've been playing hockey for twenty years and I've never seen a more biased or incompetent pair. The absolute worst. Period.

Early in the game Sweden's Number 5 kicked Ronnie Ellis. Simply kicked him. We couldn't believe nothing was done. Another thing we learned quickly: in international play the refs seldom call interference. So we'd have to protect ourselves. After this Swede kicked Ellis we were all just waiting to get him. And I was the one who happened to have the opportunity. I was skating in front of the net when the same guy interfered with me. I crosschecked him—and he fell in a heap. One of the refs gave me a penalty. While he was explaining it, Number 5 came at me again and again I crosschecked him. Only this time he fell into the referee, and they both went down. That meant a second minor penalty—only now the referee added a 10-minute misconduct. "For what?," I screamed. Suddenly the referee couldn't speak English. Someone tried to explain that under international rules you get a 10-minute misconduct for two minors. Well, I didn't know the rule and no one on Team Canada's bench did either. But we all thought that must be the rule. So I was off.

Well, it turns out there's no such rule. The next game the ref admitted to me that he'd made a mistake. I should have been off four minutes only.

While I sat those ten minutes out I really stewed. When I returned I jabbed that Number 5 with my stick every chance I got. He made circling motions with his finger around his head, as if I were crazy. The crowd loved that.

What they didn't like was our winning, 4–1. We got to the hotel after the game—and found the place being searched for bombs. Someone had told the police there was a bomb in a player's room. So we walked around Stockholm for a few hours, had some beers, and then went back to bed.

The next morning we learned that the newspapers were calling us animals and gangsters and drunkards. One guy wrote we were all sloshed on the plane to Europe. The fellow wasn't even on the plane with us, so how would he know? Sure, we had a few drinks. Who doesn't on a trans-Atlantic flight?

But I still guess we didn't impress the Swedish coach,

even though we just about killed his team in the first game. Before the second game he said he thought we'd lose every game in Russia. I think his guys wanted to make sure we did. Because it didn't take long for one of the Swedes, Ulf Sterner, to carve up Cash. The edge of his stick caught in Cash's mouth and nearly severed Wayne's tongue. This Sterner had been up in the NHL for a cup of coffee, but never impressed anyone. Yet the fans acted like he was some kind of Viking warrior. Cash went off for repairs and we all bumped and speared Sterner every chance we got. Their coach even got into the act by cursing us, until I told him that if I caught Sterner after the game I'd kill him.

All this must have really convinced the Swedes that we were animals. Everything we did on the ice was magnified. Number 5 was parading by Hadfield one time and Vic gave him an elbow for two stitches in the face. He put on a wild act, leaping and screaming and moaning all over the place for two lousy stitches. We played that game to a tie.

So we finished our short, emotional series with the Swedes. One good thing, however—the games helped us get accustomed to the wider surface. We were really rounding into shape.

Gathering up our wives and our gear, we headed for Moscow. Just as soon as we landed, one of the Russian newspapermen started asking me questions through an interpreter. How would the series go? he wanted to know. I said I hadn't brought my crystal ball along. The interpreter looked at me and the newspaperman, then shrugged his shoulders. I guess you can't translate "crystal ball" into Russian.

We got to our hotel where my first surprise came when Linda and I saw our room. It had two bunk beds. At least they were side to side; Dennis Hull said that his bunk beds were laid end to end.

When it came time to eat, the players had to be by themselves. No wives or tourists could sit with us. Because athletes in Russia are considered special, we got better food for one thing. But the wives all complained after their first meal. So here's what the NHL superstars did: we smuggled food back to the rooms for our wives.

The next day we went to see the Moscow Sports Palace. As we rode over there, I heard some of the guys complain about not playing much. I could sympathize. Throughout the series there had been talk about this. After all, Harry had thirty-five players and he could only dress half of them. But guys always grouse, even during the regular season. When we got to the arena, we were impressed. It was in beautiful shape. Weird, though, to see wire behind the cages instead of glass. Ram a puck into that wire and it rebounds clear out into center ice.

On the way to the rink I saw old women collecting garbage. At the arena several more were doing welding work. But I wasn't prepared to see them in our dressing room. There we were standing around naked, and these old ladies walked in and out as if we weren't even there. What the heck, I figured, if it doesn't bother them I won't let it bother me. It did, though.

You always hear stories about spies in Russia, and I'm pretty sure the Russians put a couple on us. Though damned if I know why. One of their trainers was a big guy we called Bulldog. He always seemed to be around observing us. And in Moscow we also noticed another huge fellow. We tagged him Bone Crusher. The Crusher had the biggest pair of hands I've ever seen. He didn't do much—just watched our dressing room. He was always there. Of course he could have been just a security guard.

At our first practice Harry called out the lines he'd be working with. I was with Parise and Rod Gilbert. Hadfield, I noticed, wasn't with anyone. He was just standing by himself. As I heard the story later, Vic had asked Harry why he wasn't teamed with anyone, and that if he couldn't play what was he doing in Russia? They had some words and Harry told him that if he didn't like it he could take off his uniform.

Parise had a few problems of his own. During scrimmage he was fighting the puck. "Hey, Phil," he said, "in that game tomorrow night just pass me the puck and watch me panic."

Later in the dressing room Vic came over. "I'm going to go, Phil," he said. "Are you sure you want to?" I asked. "Look, I've got a whole season ahead of me to play and I'm not doing any good hanging around here." So I said,

"Do what you want to do."

Honestly, I don't know what I'd have done in his situation. But I feel if you volunteer to play, you've got the right to go home. Simple as that. I don't think anyone should fault Vic or Rick Martin or Gil Perreault or Josh Guevremont who left because they weren't getting much ice time. The only real surprise was Perreault. He'd dressed for most of the games and had been doing a good job. Vic's defection didn't upset the other guys. We'd anticipated someone leaving.

Before the opening game there were ceremonies. Some young gals on figure skates gave each of us a flower. The stem broke off mine as I stood on the blue line waiting to be introduced. They called my name. I took a step and down I went. Right over that little flower stem. The Russians were trying something new to get smoother ice, skimmed milk and distilled water. Well, it sure made for an easy slide.

We found out pretty quickly that the Russians use a few different tactics when they're at home. They kicked, they speared—especially their guy Mikhailov. Still, we took a big early lead in Game Five. Until they really poured it on in the final period to stop us, 5–4.

Yet, right then we became a team. We were in a tremendous hole. The Russians had won three, tied one, and lost only once. But we were more together than ever before and in great shape.

That night I threw a party in my room. Eagleson showed up with a turkey. And the next morning there was turkey all over the place—on the walls, under my bed, in the couch. But we were relaxed.

We knew we had to keep up our fundamental play for three periods if we were going to beat them in Game Six. Number two in Moscow. And beforehand we discussed the fact that one player should always be coming back. Russia breaks as quickly as any team I've ever seen. Given a chance, they're gone.

Well, we paid attention to our game plan. We hit. We won 3–2

One more victory would tie the series. I looked upon this seventh game as the most important one we'd play. If we lost it was all over. If we won, the final game would take care of itself. I really tried to psyche myself for this game. I hadn't scored a goal in the first two. I knew the fellows were counting on me. And I don't think I've ever felt better.

In the first period I scored our two goals, I killed penalties, I played on the power play. Everything seemed to work. Then, Gary Bergman got into a tussle with Mikhailov. The guy kicked Gary three times. I wasn't exactly crazy about this fellow, particularly because he'd given me a spear earlier. So I stabbed the little runt. The ref sent me off to the penalty box and the fans booed. I held my fingers up in a V. All I meant was peace. But the fans booed even harder when they saw my fingers. While I was in the box I kept motioning to Mikhailov to come over and fight. Petrov was in his way, though, and looked at me funny. He pointed to himself as if to say, "Me?" I shouted back, "No, you jerk, not you. The other guy." Maybe the fighting had something to do with it, but we won 4–3. Now the series was tied.

The Russian officials blasted us and our "unsportsman-like" conduct. Never a word, though, about their kicking. As far as I was concerned you play hockey the way you have to in order to win. No professional wants to lose. Our style was rough, but that's what it took. The following day would tell the story.

Game Eight was 2–2 after the first period. The Russians didn't change their style—the same passing, the same kicking. But they went ahead, 5–3, after the second period. Harry told us to play positional hockey and if we got a break to take advantage of it. We had to keep them off the scoreboard. Slowly, we came back. My second goal of the night made it 5–4. Cournoyer then slammed in a pass of mine and we were tied! But the light didn't go on. Eagleson was storming. He dashed over to the goal judge. Suddenly, Alan was surrounded by Russian soldiers who tried to strong-arm him out of the place. But Pete Mahovlich saw what was going on and shouted, "They got Eagleson." We all ran over to the boards, next to the aisle where they were hassling Eagleson. The soldier released him and we hoisted him over the boards and onto the ice. As we skated him back to the safety of our bench Al said, "I've watched those Russian goal judges. When they don't want a goal to count against them, they just don't press the red-light button."

But we got the goal on the scoreboard anyway. And now the seconds were ticking away with the score tied. I went for the puck in a corner and saw Paul Henderson coming on and Pete going off. I was supposed to exit, too. But I said to myself I'm certainly not leaving at this stage. I got the puck and passed it to Henderson. He moved toward the net but a Russian put a stick between Paul's legs so he couldn't get off the shot. I came up with the puck again and took a shot. Tretiak made the save and Paul swiped at the rebound twice. The second time he put it in. There were 34 seconds left, and I knew we had the victory. It felt as sweet as the first time the Bruins won the Stanley Cup.

Well, now that it's safely over, I guess I can say I don't know what made Russia ever think they could beat us. Okay, so my tongue is poking through my cheek. But we'll be better prepared next time. And with the proper preparation, you can bet there won't be any question about who's best then. Because hockey is Canada's game. And we've got a bit of tradition going for us.

After all, hockey is our life.